DAIRY-FREE
GLUTEN-FREE
BAKING
COOKBOOK

DAiRY-FREE GLUTEN-FREE BAKING

75+ Delicious Cookies, Cakes, Pies, Breads & More

DANiELLE FAHRENKRUG

PHOTOGRAPHY BY LEIGH BEISCH

Interior and Cover Designer: Liz Cosgrove
Art Producer: Sara Feinstein
Editor: Pam Kingsley
Production Editor: Ashley Polikoff
Photography: 2019 © Leigh Beisch.
Food styling by Dan Becker.

ISBN: Print 978-1-64152-912-9 |
eBook 978-1-64152-913-6

R1

This book is dedicated to my husband, Kristopher, who encourages me to never give up, my children, Chase and Curren, and all of you who are reading this.

CONTENTS

Why Dairy-Free
AND Gluten-Free? viii

WHY DAIRY-FREE AND GLUTEN-FREE?

IF YOU ARE READING THIS BOOK, it is likely you are in a group of the 1 in 100 people worldwide with celiac disease. Or perhaps you are experiencing the common symptoms of gluten or lactose sensitivities such as digestive issues, skin disorders, bloating, and muscle cramps. Alternatively, you could be caring for a loved one with these symptoms and looking for some guidance.

Well, you're in the right place! First, it is important to know that celiac disease and nonceliac gluten sensitivity (NCGS) are autoimmune diseases that attack the villi, the small protrusions in the small intestine responsible for the absorption of vital nutrients. The damage this causes can lead to severe nutritional deficiencies and a leaky gut syndrome that could be responsible for the discomforts you may be experiencing.

You may be surprised to know that there is also a common link found between gluten intolerance and those with lactose intolerance. Celiac disease breaks down the intestinal wall and prevents the body from properly digesting the sugars found in dairy products, and because the gut is already damaged, dairy can cause the same symptoms as those associated with celiac and NCGS. It is highly important for those diagnosed with either to avoid both gluten and dairy, particularly if they are newly diagnosed, to allow their bodies to heal.

When I first transitioned to a dairy-free gluten-free diet, I was also very focused on avoiding processed gluten-free products, which was very difficult. But I knew that if I wanted to heal my body from polycystic ovarian syndrome (PCOS), I had to do it through a whole-food, natural sugar, gluten-free diet. This was challenging to say the least, as I found most breads were either hard and dense or too light and airy. It was nearly impossible to find a simple gluten-free muffin that wasn't loaded with extra salt, sugar, and fat. Plus, most baked goods also contain dairy to add moisture and depth.

As you know, cooking and baking are challenging enough, but it's considerably more difficult when you take away the gluten and dairy. I mean, who wants to go to all that work to get a flat, dense muffin or a dry cookie that crumbles in your hands?

So, I set out on a mission to figure it out. I started creating my own dairy-free gluten-free recipes that were not only easy but also tasted delicious. It took TONS of testing and trial and error, but eventually I succeeded. And like the thousands of others who have enjoyed these recipes and transformed their lives, you now also get to reap the rewards.

Throughout this book, I share my discoveries and secrets to the finest gluten-free and dairy-free baked goods, such as sourdough bread, cookies, brownies, pies, cakes, and so much more.

You've taken the first and most important step by getting this book. Now you've earned that slice of pie, so let's make it together!

THE DAIRY-FREE GLUTEN-FREE KITCHEN

Properly transitioning to a dairy-free gluten-free kitchen is key to a safe and effective healing environment. As you start your new gluten-free lifestyle, a few changes are in order to keep your home safe. Begin by thoroughly cleaning the kitchen. Everything should be taken out of cupboards, refrigerators, drawers, and cabinets and cleaned thoroughly with nontoxic cleaner before putting gluten-free items in place. Any food items with gluten should be stored in their own cabinets separate from gluten-free items. There should also be appliances and tools (such as wooden spoons and cutting boards that have pores where gluten can stick) specifically designated for gluten-free products to assure no cross contamination. Even a small contact with gluten or dairy can cause major discomfort.

WHAT IS GLUTEN AND WHAT DOES IT DO?

Gluten is a protein found in some grains. The two main proteins in gluten are gliadin and glutenin. When they come in contact with water, these proteins link and become gluten strands that build a web-like network. This substance becomes the "glue" that holds foods together and gives it stretch, elasticity, and beloved texture. This protein is found in grains such as wheat (including durum, semolina, kamut, spelt, einkorn, triticale, and farro), barley, rye, and oats (unless the oats are certified gluten-free).

Gluten-related disorders are adverse reactions to the gluten protein. The level of sensitivity can range from a mild intolerance, which does not involve any antibodies, to celiac disease, in which the immune system attacks itself in response to eating gluten and prevents the body from properly absorbing food. Symptoms include bloating, diarrhea, infertility, osteoporosis, anemia, malnutrition, and neurological disorders, to name a few.

Gluten was originally used back in the early 20th century as a food stabilizer, giving treats such as ice cream the density needed to prevent melting when handled by a customer. Today, it is used in most baked goods such as bread, pasta, crackers, muffins, pies, cakes, and pastries. Even unsuspecting items—soy sauce, salad dressing, soup, candy, toothpaste, shampoo, cleaning products, supplements, food coloring, Play-Doh, and beauty products—can ambush the unaware person with doses of gluten—isn't that crazy?

GLUTEN PROVIDES STRUCTURE AND VOLUME

Don't you just love sinking your teeth into a fluffy bagel without having it feel dense or flat or crumble in our hands? You can thank gluten for that. As gluten molecules stick together, they become stronger. This is especially important during fermentation. The reason bakers fold resting dough or "punch" the dough during resting time is to allow gluten strands to align and remove some of the gas bubbles formed by the yeast during rising. The release of gas is what makes baked goods fluffy and airy.

The way gluten reacts in baked goods varies. Fat from butters and oils coat the protein strands of gluten, which slows down the binding process.

Lean breads such as sandwich breads have less fat and can stretch and rise more, creating light and airy bread.

The key to structure and volume in baked goods is making sure the flours are thoroughly moistened. The more the flour is moistened, the better it can rise. Gluten-free dough can become tough, since it absorbs liquid quickly. The key to helping dough rise is using lots of liquid and binding agents, so the dough is very wet and sticky.

Gluten is essential for the flour to hold in moisture. When gluten bonds form, they give elasticity and stretch to traditional dough by trapping gasses, which supports leavening (making the dough rise). Ever eat a gluten-free pastry or sandwich bread that is crumbly and falls apart? It's not the most satisfying experience! Gluten retains water, which prevents breads, muffins, and cakes from drying out as soon as they are cut or removed from the oven. That is why some gluten-free baked goods can be dry and flaky—they need the gluten to retain moisture, unless you use the right formula.

GLUTEN-FREE BAKING FLOUR BLENDS

One summer I was working on creating gluten-free oatmeal cookies for our Fourth of July party, which resulted in flat cookies that baked into each other. What I realized quickly is the flours I was using were too moist. I needed less of the light starch I was using and more dense flour. The most common complaints about gluten-free baked goods are that the hearty breads are too dense or tasteless, cookies and sandwich breads crumble, and piecrusts fall apart or are rubbery.

The culprit is the absence of gluten. Gluten is what gives baked goods the leavening and proper air flow to make them light and fluffy and maintain the right amount of moisture. In gluten-free baking, this consistency cannot be achieved by a simple substitution. Rather, you need a tried-and-true formula created by fine-tuning different gluten-free flours into blends that hold the necessary structure and moisture without gluten—it can be done.

It is time to reinvent grandmom's Italian pizza dough, mom's famous biscuits, birthday cakes used for every celebration, the husband's much-loved

CONTINUED ON PAGE 6

GLUTEN-FREE FLOURS

INGREDIENT	DESCRIPTION	CHARACTERISTICS IN BAKING, PRO AND CON
Almond meal or flour	Almond meal or flour is made from finely ground almonds and provides a sweet flavor to baked goods.	Almond meal or flour is great to add to cakes and muffins, as it holds moisture well and is a good substitute for wheat. It may need an extra binding agent, such as egg, in baking applications. It is high in protein, fiber, and healthy fats. Go for "blanched" almond meal or flour, which has no skins and leaves a more neutral taste in baked goods and cookies.
Amaranth flour	Amaranth flour is derived from the seeds of the amaranth plant and was an ancient flour used by the Aztecs. This flour has a mildly nutty flavor and helps baked goods brown.	This flour is high in protein, fiber, and lysine, an essential amino acid. Eating raw amaranth grains or flour can prevent the body from absorbing nutrients, so it is best to use this in baked goods rather than no-bake goods.
Coconut flour	Coconut flour is great for baked goods, as it adds natural sweetness. It is extremely nutritious, low carb, and packed with fiber.	It does not substitute for wheat, as it is a denser flour, and mixtures that use it may need more liquid or less flour in baking.
Corn flour and cornmeal	Corn flour is finely ground and wonderful to use in breads, cakes, and pancakes. Cornmeal is coarsely ground and commonly used for making corn bread, crusts, breading, and polenta. It naturally provides a slightly sweet flavor to baked goods.	Corn flour gives depth and structure to baked goods and works best when combined with a binding agent, such as egg, to help it hold shape.
Garbanzo bean flour	Garbanzo bean flour, also known as besan, gram, or chickpea flour, is derived from grinding raw chickpeas. It is naturally gluten-free and rich in protein, fiber, and other vitamins and minerals.	Garbanzo bean flour works well in baking when combined with other gluten-free flours. Alone, it works well as a binder in veggie burgers and fritters. It is also great for making thin pancakes such as crepes.
Buckwheat flour	Buckwheat is a fruit that is dried and formed into a flour. It is *not* a type of wheat, despite the name. It has a strong, robust flavor and is high in protein, fiber, and B vitamins.	Very dense and heavy, buckwheat flour mixes well with light starches, like tapioca flour or arrowroot.
Flaxseed meal	Flaxseed meal is ground flaxseed that has a light flour consistency. It is high in fiber and omega-3 fatty acids.	Flaxseed meal works well in baking, as it adds moisture and assists in binding flours together. It can also be combined with warm water as an egg replacer.

INGREDIENT	DESCRIPTION	CHARACTERISTICS IN BAKING, PRO AND CON
Masa harina	Not to be confused with corn flour, masa harina is made from finely ground corn kernels that have been soaked in limewater, or calcium hydroxide.	Commonly used to make tortillas, tamales, and pupusas in Mexican dishes where the baked good does not need to rise.
Millet flour	Millet is an ancient grain with a mildly sweet, nutty flavor and is rich in nutrients.	Millet has a strong flavor and works best in baking when combined with other gluten-free flours.
Oat flour	Oats can be ground into a fine powder that is high in fiber, protein, and iron. They add wonderful structure to cookies, muffins, quick breads, and pancakes. Make sure they are labeled certified gluten-free, as some oats are cross-contaminated with wheat when they are grown side by side.	Oats soak up loads of moisture, so when used in baking, extra liquid may be necessary.
Quinoa flour	Quinoa flour is an incredibly nutrient-rich and moist gluten-free flour milled from a grain native to the Andes Mountains in South America. It is rich in B vitamins, amino acids, and fiber.	Quinoa flour has a nutty flavor that can overpower baked goods. It is best when mixed with other gluten-free flours.
Rice flour	Rice flour is the most common gluten-free flour and can be found in most store-bought mixes. It comes from three sources: brown rice, sweet white rice, and white rice.	Rice flour is a heavy flour, and more water may be required when using it in baking. It mixes best with other gluten-free flours and light starches.
Sorghum flour	Sorghum flour, also known as milo and jowar, can be found in red and white varieties. It has a slightly sweet flavor and is high in fiber and protein.	Sorghum flour is dense and works best in baking when combined with other gluten-free flours.
Teff flour	Teff flour is a staple in Ethiopia and is available in dark and light varieties. It aids circulation and weight loss and is packed with calcium, phosphorus (helps balance hormones naturally), fiber, and protein. The flavor is mildly nutty.	Works well in pancakes, waffles, and quick breads when mixed with other gluten-free flours.
Tigernut flour	Despite its name, tigernut is not a nut, as it is derived from a root vegetable. It is grain-free and gluten-free and is starting to become more popular in the United States.	This flour is naturally sweet, so less sugar is needed when using it in baking.

CONTINUED FROM PAGE 3

carrot cake, double crusted pies, peach cobbler, and even homemade dinner rolls.

How is this possible? Because there are tricks of the trade: ratios of wet to dry ingredients, knowing how to bind flours with other flours, adding natural fruits that hold ingredients together, and the type and amount of fats to use. And it all starts with the flours.

GLUTEN-FREE FLOUR

Plant-derived flours work together the same way their original plant forms did. They either build each other up or down. God gave us an abundance of plants for a reason. Not only do they heal and help us grow, but they work together to ensure we eat all the right nutrients as intended. No one plant has everything we need to survive, but if we eat a variety, we get what we need.

We are blessed to have grocery stores with a readily available variety of gluten-free flours. The most common plant-derived flours are made from almonds, rice, quinoa, garbanzo beans, coconuts, and bananas. The secret to using these flours is how they mix together. Just as you can't mix oil with water and hope their compounds blend together, you can't mix two dense flours like coconut and rice and hope for a moist muffin. Use the gluten-free flours chart on pages 4 and 5 as a gauge for the density of gluten-free alternatives.

These gluten-free flours are also healthier than white flours because they are much more nutrient dense, containing vital amounts of amino acids, protein, fiber, vitamins, and minerals.

STARCHES

Root vegetables are well tolerated by people with a gluten intolerance. They are excellent gluten-free foods that can be used as natural thickening agents in place of flour. Starches can be used to thicken soups and stews, pie fillings, and sauces. They are a lighter and less dense than some flours, such as coconut and buckwheat flour, and work well in baking when combined with dense flours; they are what keep gluten-free baked goods light. However, they are too light to survive the weight of heavy liquids on their own. Combine them with heavy flours to achieve the proper texture in your baked goods.

Arrowroot

Arrowroot mixes well with gluten-free flour mix, coconut flour, and buckwheat flour, as it adds lightness. It is also good for thickening soups and sauces. I like to add arrowroot to my basic gluten-free flour mix to provide a light and airy texture.

Cornstarch

Cornstarch, also known as corn flour, is extracted from the endosperm of corn. It is an ingredient commonly used in baking powder as the filler, which works to help food rise after liquid is added. Cornstarch is also used to thicken soups, pie filling, and sauces.

Potato Starch

Potato starch or flour is made from dehydrated potatoes and is a light and very fine powder that is high in fiber and protein. It adds structure to gluten-free baking, lending a soft, chewy consistency to homemade breads, pizza crust, and baked goods. Potato starch works best when mixed with other gluten-free flours, as it cannot hold its own in baked goods.

Tapioca Flour

Tapioca starch or flour is made from the cassava plant. It is a light powder that mixes well with heavy gluten-free flours such as rice flour, buckwheat, and coconut flour. It naturally helps to bind foods, making baked goods hold their shape. It is slightly sweet and is good for thickening soups and sauces. In baking, make sure not to use too much tapioca flour, as it can cause baked goods and sauces to have a chewy or rubbery texture since it also acts as a binding agent in gluten-free recipes.

BINDERS

Binders are essential elements in gluten-free baking. Since gluten is the "glue" that holds traditional baked goods together, it must be replaced. Popular binding agents in baked goods include eggs, flaxseed, psyllium husk, chia seeds, guar gum, and xanthan gum.

Guar Gum

Guar gum, which comes from a legume plant, has been used for centuries as a thickener and stabilizer in food and medicine. It works well in gluten-free baking to hold the texture and structure of baked goods. It is also commonly found in prepared almond milk, coconut milk, yogurts, body lotions, and fiber supplements. When digested, guar gum is fermented to short-chain fatty acids that do not appear to be absorbed by the gut. So basically, it passes quickly. The downside is some people may experience gut-related discomfort from guar gum, including abdominal pain, cramps, diarrhea, and excess gas.

Xanthan Gum

A synthetic binder, xanthan gum is a polysaccharide (a carbohydrate) that is extracted from the bacteria *Xanthomonas campestris*. Dried and turned into powder, it is used in gluten-free cookies, muffins, cakes, breads, and pizza crust, as it helps improve texture, consistency, and taste. Xanthan gum can also thicken syrup, ice cream, creamy salad dressings, and candy. The most common side effect of xanthan gum is an upset stomach caused by an altering of the gut bacteria. This can lead to increased bowel movements and loose stools. If you experience these symptoms from these binders, just remove the ingredient from the recipe and substitute it with 1 tablespoon psyllium husk powder.

CERTIFIED GLUTEN-FREE

Gluten has seeped into every possible nook and cranny of the consumer market, including shampoos and toothpaste. Finding wheat on food labels has become much easier since the Food Allergen Labeling and Consumer Protection Act (FALCPA) became a law in 2004. It requires that the top eight allergens, including wheat, be clearly identified on labels containing them.

But that's not enough. Oats are naturally gluten-free but can end up containing gluten if grown alongside wheat or processed in a plant or mill that also processes gluten-containing grains. Always scan the label of such products for the "certified gluten-free" logo, which ensures the product hasn't been processed using the same machinery used for wheat products.

HOMEMADE GLUTEN-FREE FLOUR BLENDS

For years I would buy gluten-free flour blends and start adding my own starches to it to soften the blend. Some of these would turn out dry and heavy when I used them in my recipes. Other times, the recipe would turn out fine when I used a different blend. And then other blends would add wonderful moisture, but they contained dairy. So in the end, I developed my own blends.

These are my go-to flour blends—they will make baking easy for you, yielding consistent results every time. But remember, there is no one-size-fits-all solution when it comes to baking. For that reason, I am including several different blends, based on the type of baked good each one works best with. Many (though not all) of the recipes in the book will call for one of them.

Now, you may feel overwhelmed at the thought of having to make these blends, but I assure you they are effortless to create once you have the ingredients. The ingredients can easily be found online at Amazon and Thrive Market, and at most specialty grocery stores. And the recipes make large batches, so you don't have to make them for every recipe. Make more than you need, store it tightly sealed, and you are good to go!

WEIGHT VS. VOLUME MEASUREMENT

Understanding the difference between weight and volume measurements in baking can make all the difference in the result. The weight of nuts is far different from that of marshmallows for the same volume measure. Also, when measuring flours and sugars by volume, the weight can vary depending on if the flour or sugar is packed tightly or loosely in a measuring cup. Weight measure is preferable when making these blends, and it's super easy after you invest in a scale.

If volume measure is your ticket, the proper method is key. First, make sure you are using dry measuring cups. Second, don't measure directly over the bowl. For flour, lightly spoon it into the measuring cup until it is overflowing the cup. Using the back of a knife, slide it across the top rim of the cup to level it.

When measuring liquid ingredients such as water, milk, or oil, use a liquid measuring cup. Set it on a flat surface or counter and fill to the measurement needed. Check it at eye level to make sure it is exact.

Basic Gluten-Free Flour Blend

NUT-FREE, SOY-FREE, VEGAN
PREP TIME: 5 MINUTES MAKES 7¼ CUPS

This is a quick and easy all-purpose gluten-free flour blend to substitute one-to-one for wheat flour.

2 cups brown rice flour
(11.5 ounces)

2 cups white rice flour (11.5 ounces)

1 cup tapioca flour (4.3 ounces)

1 cup potato starch (5.64 ounces)

¾ cup sorghum flour (3.2 ounces)

½ cup arrowroot (2.26 ounces)

1 tablespoon xanthan gum

In a large bowl, whisk together all the ingredients until well blended.

STORAGE: Store at room temperature in an airtight container, preferably glass, in a cool, dry place.

SUBSTITUTIONS: If avoiding nightshades, use cornstarch instead of potato starch. If avoiding xanthan gum, use an equal amount of guar gum or powdered gelatin.

Gluten-Free Cake and Pastry Flour Blend

SOY-FREE, VEGAN
PREP TIME: 5 MINUTES MAKES 5½ CUPS

This is a light and moist flour blend to use when making cakes. Use as a one-to-one substitute for wheat flour.

2 cups sweet white rice flour (11.15 ounces)

2 cups almond meal (6.77 ounces)

1½ cups potato starch (8.47 ounces)

1 tablespoon xanthan gum

In a large bowl, whisk together all the ingredients until well blended.

PREP TIP: If there are clumps in the mixture, put it through a sifter.

STORAGE: Store at room temperature in an airtight container, preferably glass, in a cool, dry place.

SUBSTITUTIONS: If avoiding nightshades, use cornstarch instead of potato starch. If avoiding xanthan gum, use an equal amount of guar gum or powdered gelatin.

Gluten-Free Whole-Grain Flour Blend

NUT-FREE, SOY-FREE, VEGAN
PREP TIME: 5 MINUTES MAKES 4 CUPS

A quick and easy gluten-free flour blend filled with heart-healthy whole grains.

1 cup sweet white rice flour (5.89 ounces)

1 cup millet flour (4.2 ounces)

½ cup flaxseed meal (2.96 ounces)

½ cup tapioca flour (2.15 ounces)

½ cup garbanzo bean flour (1.62 ounces)

½ cup potato starch (2.82 ounces)

½ teaspoons xanthan gum

In a large bowl, whisk together all the ingredients until well blended.

STORAGE: Store at room temperature in a large airtight container, preferably glass, in a cool, dry place.

SUBSTITUTIONS: If avoiding nightshades, use cornstarch instead of potato starch. If avoiding xanthan gum, use an equal amount of guar gum or powdered gelatin.

READY-MADE GLUTEN-FREE FLOUR BLENDS

My blends provide the best results, but I understand the convenience of buying ready-made gluten-free flour mixes. Here you will find the top five brands I have tried and had success with, in order of preference.

Bob's Red Mill Gluten-Free 1-to-1 Baking Flour: This mix has always worked well in cookies and quick breads. In fact, it is the foundation of the ingredients I use in my own homemade basic gluten-free flour blend. Depending on the recipe, I will add a starch, such as extra potato starch or tapioca flour, to offset other ingredients and provide a fluffier consistency. Use whenever a recipe calls for my basic gluten-free flour blend.

Krusteaz Gluten-Free All-Purpose Flour Mix: I like the combination of high protein quinoa and millet in this mix, which is helpful for the yeast to rise in breads. Use whenever a recipe calls for my gluten-free flour blend or cake and pastry blend.

Pamela's Gluten-Free Artisan Blend Flour: This is a basic mix to use one-to-one in recipes that call for my blends or wheat flour.

King Arthur Flour Gluten-Free Measure for Measure Flour: This is a simple blend similar to my all-purpose blend. This is a good one-to-one substitute in cookie recipes.

Authentic Foods Gluten-Free Multi-Blend Flour: This blend has a nice mix of light and airy flours to keep baked goods fluffy.

Each of these works well as a one-to-one alternative when my basic gluten-free flour mix is called in a recipe.

DAIRY-FREE BAKING

Getting rid of dairy in baked goods while maintaining the expected viscosity and texture is one of the hardest accomplishments in dairy-free gluten-free baking.

Dairy generally plays a huge role in batters and dough, just like peanut butter and jelly go together. You just can't have one without the other. Or can you?

My grandmother's version of a delicious bread loaf contains milk, eggs, honey, water, salt, and yeast. Milk helps breads rise and provides a crisp crust. Milk is especially important in bread machine breads because it gives baked goods structure, strength, and a satisfying flavor. The protein in milk helps the dough withstand rising during the baking process. The sugar and fat in milk help tenderize and moisten the baked good while adding flavor. Sugar in milk creates a crispy golden-brown crust on baked goods.

But is it healthy to avoid dairy in your diet? Yes, it is. Just look at the Mediterranean diet, which is highly valued as one of the healthiest ways to eat. It is a diet rich in plants and omega 3 fatty acids from almonds, olive oil, and seafood. Dairy is rarely incorporated, except for the occasional yogurt and hard cheese. Luckily for anyone on a gluten-free diet, there are dairy-free almond and coconut milks, yogurts, and butters made from heart-healthy oils such as olive oil and avocado oil. These dairy-free swaps are essential for adding moisture to quick breads and cookies.

Having dairy-free items in your pantry helps make baking a breeze. You do not have to have all these ingredients on hand, but these are the ones most commonly used in my recipes. Many people have one or two favorite dairy-free milks, so try out a few to determine which ones best suit your tastes.

THE DAIRY-FREE PANTRY

INGREDIENT	DESCRIPTION	CHARACTERISTICS IN BAKING, PRO AND CON
Nut milk (almond, cashew, coconut)	Nut milk is a term to describe a thick milk-like liquid that is made from nuts by soaking them in water, crushing and blending them, and then straining the liquid.	Nut milk works well whenever dairy milk is called for in a recipe. It is especially good in baked oatmeal, puddings, cookies, and quick breads, as it adds a delicious amount of moisture. Choose unsweetened or original-flavor varieties for baking.
Canned coconut milk	Canned coconut milk is close to the creaminess of dairy milk. It is made from shredded coconut flesh combined with water that is then strained to create a creamy, sweet, rich, and slightly sweet liquid. Available in low- and full-fat varieties, canned coconut milk separates when canned and should be shaken before using. The low-fat variety has more separation than the full-fat.	Use full-fat coconut milk as an alternative to dairy whipped cream. Chill a can of it upside down in the refrigerator. Flip over when ready to use, open, and then drain the water. Beat the cream on high until a whipped cream consistency is formed. It will have a coconut flavor. You will also want to add a bit of confectioners' sugar and vanilla extract to sweeten it for a delicious creamy blend.
Oat milk	Oat milk is made by soaking oats in water, blending them in a blender or food processor, and then straining the liquid.	Oat milk is very creamy and delicious! It works well as a substitute for dairy in baking.
Hemp milk	Hemp milk is made by soaking hemp seeds in water, blending them in a blender or food processor, and then straining the liquid.	Hemp milk has a texture similar to cow's milk. it works well as a substitute for dairy in baking and provides lots of moisture.
Flax milk	Flax milk is made by soaking flaxseed in water, blending them in a blender or food processor, and then straining the liquid.	Flax milk is creamy and delicious! Use as a substitute for dairy in baking.
Soy milk	Soy milk is made by soaking soy beans in water, blending them in a blender or food processor, and then straining the liquid.	Soy milk is creamy and delicious! It works well as a substitute for dairy in baking.
Rice milk	Rice milk is made by soaking rice grains in water, blending them in a blender or food processor, and then straining the liquid. The consistency is much thinner than nut milk, oat, and hemp milk.	Rice milk is very light. It works well as a substitute in recipes for pancakes that call for milk.

INGREDIENT	DESCRIPTION	CHARACTERISTICS IN BAKING, PRO AND CON
Olive oil	Olive oil is made by pressing whole olives and straining the oil. It is commonly used in cooking, baking, and salad dressings.	Olive oil works to add moisture, particularly in recipes for breads. It aids in moistening the dough.
Avocado oil	Avocado oil is an edible oil pressed from the fleshy pulp surrounding the avocado pit and not the pit itself. It can withstand high heat.	Avocado oil works to add moisture, particularly in breads, cakes, and quick breads. It aids in moistening the dough.
Coconut oil	Coconut oil is the oil pressed from the kernel or meat of mature coconuts.	Coconut oil adds moisture, particularly in recipes for cookies and brownies as a substitute for butter. It adds moisture and sweetness to baked goods.
Dairy-free yogurt alternative	There are several varieties of yogurt made with different of types of dairy-free milk, such as soy yogurt, flax yogurt, almond yogurt, cashew yogurt, and coconut yogurt. They are creamy and packed with protein and probiotics.	Dairy-free yogurts work well in baking. You can substitute them one-to-one for regular yogurt. In baking, it helps create a moist baked good.
Vegan butter	Vegan butter is a butter or spread made from vegetable oils. It comes in many forms such as in tubs, sticks, or whipped. It can be soy-free, olive oil based, coconut based, and even flavored with garlic and herbs.	Butter is a natural thickener. Since dairy butter is off-limits, vegan butter makes a good substitute, as it is lactose-free and dairy-free. Readily available in grocery stores, it bakes like butter and can be substituted equally.

TROUBLESHOOTING YOUR BAKED GOODS

It is not uncommon to encounter hiccups when first starting out with dairy-free gluten-free baking. Cookies can turn out dense and hard, breads may not rise, and muffin tops can be flat. It happens, but knowing how to adjust for these results is the key to successful baking. Occasionally the culprit is as simple as an ingredient being too cold or warm. For example, when a recipe calls for room temperature butter, the stick should be soft enough to hold an indention when you press it with your finger but not too soft that it loses its shape. Dairy-free butter tends to get to room temperature quickly, so it will not need as much time to soften as regular butter. These simple tips will help you on your culinary journey and make baking easier.

CAKES, MUFFINS, AND CUPCAKES

Every baked good has its own method or "chemistry" of how it reacts with other ingredients. It matters what the ratio of wet to dry ingredients is, what type of fat is used, and whether the fat is solid or liquid. Cakes, muffins, and cupcakes happen to be my favorite gluten-free things to make. They are less challenging than yeast breads and cakes. But you may still end up with a muffin that is flat on top, sinks in, or is chewy or dense. Here is how we can work to fix those issues.

✱ Too dry, crumbly, chewy, or dense

If your cake, muffin, or cupcake is dry, increase the liquid by 1 to 4 tablespoons or add an egg (equal to about ¼ cup). If it is crumbly, it may need more of binding agent. A crumbly texture may also be a sign of under- or overcooking due to improper oven temperature. Use an oven thermometer to determine if your oven runs hot or cold, and have it repaired or adjust the oven setting to be closer to the correct temperature. If your baked good is chewy or dense, increase the baking time by 5 to 10 minutes or adjust the wet and dry ingredients by decreasing the liquid or increasing the flour by 1 tablespoon at a time.

✱ Did not rise

This can be caused by old baking powder or baking soda, or from not using enough of these leavening agents in the recipe. Make sure your ingredients have not expired, and replace them every six months. Otherwise, they lose their potency and stop working. If it's not the age of the leavening, try adjusting the measurements. Start by increasing the baking powder or baking soda by ⅛ to ¼ teaspoon.

✱ Cake "fell" / not enough structure

If your cake sinks or your muffins have flat tops and increasing baking time does not work, increase the flour by 1 tablespoon to ½ cup. Cakes can also "fall" if you open the oven door at a crucial rise time. Use an oven light to see the baked good so you are not tempted to open the door. For muffins, make sure not to overmix the batter, which can make them tough.

✱ Overly moist layer at top or bottom / sticks to the pan with a greasy texture

Be sure to measure oil and butter carefully. Decrease the oil or butter by 1 to 2 tablespoons.

✱ Overbaked exterior and underbaked interior

This is a possible sign that the oven temperature is too high. Lower the oven temperature and extend the baking time. Make sure not to open the oven during baking. Check the bake by turning on an oven light instead. Double-check that ingredients like flours and sugars are measured properly with a kitchen scale or by using the back-of-knife leveling method.

A NOTE ABOUT SUGAR AND SALT

An important factor in healing the gut and body is avoiding processed foods. To make things simpler for you, I suggest using organic sugar, which is not as processed as white sugar is and still contains traces of nutrition from molasses. I also call for coconut sugar as an alternative to regular white sugar or brown sugar, but you can use brown sugar if the other is too expensive. You'll also see maple syrup and honey called for in some of the recipes. Again, I choose these for their health benefits; they offer more nutritional value, such as providing antioxidants, improving digestion, and helping protect skin health.

Personally, in my own life, I use monk fruit or birch xylitol in place of white sugar, and coconut sugar in place of brown sugar. They won't spike blood sugar levels the same way white sugar does.

Note that I tested these recipes using standard table salt unless otherwise specified. Sometimes I call for kosher salt when a coarser grain is needed, such as when a recipe calls for a finishing sprinkle.

PIECRUSTS

When I first started making piecrust with gluten-free flours, I tried to get really fancy with it and ended up with a crust that was chewy and hard, not flaky and buttery like a crust is meant to be. You could knock on the top of the pie and hear it echo back! Luckily, practice makes perfect, and you will find perfection in this book's gluten-free piecrust recipe. Following are piecrust tips that will help you achieve this success as well.

✳ Dough is tough, dry, and hard to work with

Dry dough may be a result of needing more liquid. Increase the water by 1 tablespoon at a time until the dough is easier to work with. Make sure not to forget the vinegar. This is the secret ingredient to keep the crust from getting tough.

✳ Crust has a crumbly texture

If the piecrust is crumbly, it may need more liquid or a binder, such as xanthan gum, flaxseed meal, or psyllium husks.

✳ Crust is not flaky

Make sure to cut the butter properly into the flour, and also make sure that all ingredients are cold. Add a small amount of apple cider vinegar, which helps soften baked goods in gluten-free baking.

✳ Crust is burnt along the edge or on top

If the edges start to burn, wrap the edges of the pie with aluminum foil or a piecrust shield. This will allow the center to stay open to release moisture and cook without the edges burning. If the entire top of the pie is browning too quickly, tent the pie with foil to continue cooking.

TIPS TO ENSURE THE PERFECT CRUST

Use lactose-free vegan butter as a natural thickener, making sure it is very chilled. After the dough is formed, wrap it in plastic wrap and chill it thoroughly before rolling out to ensure it holds its shape. Right before baking, always make sure to cut vents in the top crust of the pie, if you have one. A pie needs to let steam escape during baking to keep the crust from getting soggy. A pie is ready when the crust is golden brown and the juices start to bubble up in the center. When baking a fruit pie, let it cool completely before cutting to allow the filling time to set.

COOKIES AND BARS

Cookies and bars are brilliant to bring to celebrations or enjoy for snacks. They are quick to make and, if using the right ingredients, can be healthy. Occasionally, there can be issues—particularly due to altitude, oven problems, or undermixed batter—that cause a flat or burnt treat. Here's how to prevent issues.

* Dough is greasy

If the batter is overly greasy, use less butter or oil. Too much oil can create a thin or dense cookie.

* Dough spread in the oven / cookies are flat

Sometimes this is due to not enough flour or the need for a binder. Make sure all ingredients are measured properly and leavening ingredients are not expired. Add 1 to 2 tablespoons more flour to the batter. You can also chill the dough for about 30 minutes to solidify the fat, so it spreads less in the oven.

✳ Cookies lack flavor

Drop cookies taste best when the dough has been chilled for 30 minutes before shaping. Sometimes, time is of the essence and you just need to get them in the oven, and that's fine. But if time is not an issue, take the time to cover the bowl and let the batter chill. This allows all the flavors to develop, the cookies to brown better, and as mentioned on page 21, it prevents them from spreading too thin.

✳ Cookies didn't bake evenly / edges are dark but middles are underbaked

The oven temperature is too high. Turn the temperature down 25°F and cook it slightly longer.

🍰 NUT BUTTERS

What kind of peanut butter or nut butter is healthiest? Natural peanut butter should be used because it contains only peanuts—and no added ingredients like hydrogenated oils, soy protein, corn syrup, stabilizers, and fillers. It also contains less salt. Choose organic peanut butter, preferably one made with Valencia peanuts because they do not grow where there is mold, like traditional ones. If you have a peanut allergy, use seed butter or another nut butter such as cashew or almond butter in its place.

Besides reading the label, which is important, you can tell nut butters are natural because they typically have oil at the top of the jar. I choose to drain this off before using—no need to add more oil that's not necessary.

BREADS

Breads are one of the hardest gluten-free baked goods to make. Since gluten-free flours do not have the binding protein that helps them rise, they need other agents to do the work. I suggest keeping the dough very moist and wet during the leavening process, to allow gas and airflow to develop. That is one of the best tips to ensure a fluffy sandwich bread or roll. Use the rest of these tips to resolve any issues.

✳ Dough didn't rise

Three main factors for breads not rising are the yeast is bad, the water mixed to activate the yeast is too hot or too cold (it should be lukewarm), or there is too much flour, which weighs the mixture down during the leavening process.

✳ Bread is dry

Decrease the amount of flour and increase liquid until the dough is soft and elastic.

It is important to allow the dough to rise only until double in size. If the dough is used before rising is complete, it will be denser. If it over-expands, it may flatten during baking. Rising time may vary depending on altitude levels; less rise time is needed at higher altitudes.

✳ Bread has large holes throughout

Punch down the dough twice during the rising process. This releases air and gas and brings sugars and moisture back to a cohesive form.

✳ Bread has a dense crumb

Add psyllium husk to the batter as a binder in place of some of the flour, or replace some of the flour with cornstarch or potato starch to lighten it up.

FAQS ABOUT GLUTEN-FREE DAIRY-FREE BAKING

* I am new to baking. Where do I start?

How exciting for you! Baking is a form of chemistry, where everything works in sync and the correct measurements must be used. The tools you will use most frequently are mixing bowls of all sizes, spatulas, whisks, measuring spoons, measuring cups for dry ingredients, and a measuring cup for liquid. You will also want to invest in a stand or a hand-held mixer, food processor, and blender. You do not need to feel overwhelmed about baking pans—simply get a few basics:

- **Baking sheets** (at least 2)
- **Loaf pan** (9-inch)
- **Muffin pan** (12-cup)
- **Pie pan** (9-inch)
- **Rectangular pan** (9-by-13-inch)
- **Round cake pan** (9-inch)
- **Silicone baking mat** (to prevent cookies from burning on the bottom)
- **Square cake pan** (9-inch)
- **Wire cooling racks**

* What if I can't find these gluten-free flours at my local grocery store?

The good news is gluten-free flours are readily available online. If you cannot find them at your grocery store, you can purchase them and have them delivered to you.

* What if I don't have the time?

Taking control of your health is important, and we should always make the time for that. If time is an issue, start small. Start by making a batch of cookies and freeze half the dough to use at another time. That way, you have homemade cookie dough available to bake and eat in less than 15 minutes. Make a double batch of muffins, and freeze half for busy mornings.

✱ Can I use a premade gluten-free mix?

Yes, see my favorites on page 12 or try other brands—just make sure they are also dairy-free.

✱ Do I have to use the exact ingredients you say to use?

Yes and no. Would you trust a builder to build your home using paper straws instead of bricks? Of course not—I am pretty sure it would blow over or crumble and fall. The same works for baking. Changing a few ingredients could be the difference between a perfect cookie and one that is flat or too crispy. I recommend following the ingredients and any substitutions that are suggested, unless you are a pretty savvy baker and understand how the ingredients will work together.

These are a few common things that you may use as substitutions in these recipes:

- **To replace yogurt:** use unsweetened applesauce
- **To replace potato starch:** use cornstarch
- **To replace xanthan gum:** use an equal amount of guar gum, carob (locust bean) gum, or gelatin (use powdered form)
- **To replace 1 large egg (¼ cup):** use egg replacer or flaxseed meal "egg." To make, combine 1 tablespoon flaxseed meal with 3 tablespoons hot water. Stir and let stand for 10 minutes until it has thickened.
- **To replace coconut oil's strong flavor:** use refined coconut oil

✱ Gluten-free + dairy-free = expensive. What if it doesn't fit in my budget?

We are talking about your health, and nothing is more priceless than taking care of yourself. Gluten-free flours are more expensive than white flours, but in the long run, your body will be fueled with the proper nutrients. Plant flours can have more vitamins, minerals, protein, and fiber to help keep your health in check. Also, eating a healthy diet may help keep medical bills down. Your gut will thank you for that one.

Shop for flours in bulk and online. Keep an eye out for sales, and when they do happen, stock up on the ingredients you need. The good news is dairy-free milk is about the same price as dairy milk.

✱ Isn't it difficult? I don't think I can do this . . .

Once you start baking, it becomes a practice that you will soon perfect. Like anything, practice makes perfect. I am here with you, and I believe in you.

✱ I've tried gluten-free, and it doesn't taste good. How is this different?

Many store-bought products must have preservatives to increase their shelf life. Those preservatives can give a rancid taste to items, and baked goods made with them can lose their flavor over time. In this book, I call for only fresh, real ingredients that taste best when consumed within one to three days.

✱ Can this truly help me?

Yes! Eating gluten-free and dairy-free allows time for your gut to heal and find balance again. This time also frees your mind to function more clearly, as it is not working on processing white carbohydrates and sugars. Instead, it is utilizing the nutrients in these flours to help you thrive. Time to say goodbye to a bloated stomach and that sluggish feeling after eating. You will be amazed how incredible you will feel after removing gluten and dairy from your diet.

✱ Where can I find affordable gluten-free/dairy-free ingredients?

My top money-saving places are Amazon, Thrive Market, Sprouts (they have a great bulk section), Aldi, Grocery Outlet (occasionally carries coconut sugar and gluten-free flours), and Costco.

HIGH-ALTITUDE BAKING

The adjustments listed here are suggestions to make when baking in different altitudes. A common high-altitude issue is that moisture evaporates more quickly than when baking at low altitude. Baked goods using yeast, baking powder, baking soda, and egg whites may rise well and then fall. Since baking at high altitude tends to take longer, I suggest making one recipe as instructed at a time and testing it to see if the texture and appearance are acceptable. If it is not, try the recipe again with my suggestions until the recipe works for you.

At high altitude:

* Due to the drier air, liquids evaporate faster, so amounts of flour, sugar, and liquids may need to be adjusted to prevent batter from becoming dry, sticky, or too moist.

* The air pressure is lower, so most foods take longer to bake. Increase the oven temperature by 20°F or bake about 10 minutes longer at the recommended temperature.

* For cakes leavened by air, such as angel food cake, beat the egg whites to soft peaks, and do not overmix. For other baked goods, leavening agents such as baking soda, baking powder, and yeast may need to be decreased. Reduce by ⅛ to ¼ teaspoon at a time as needed. Yeast doughs may need less time to rise and may need to be "punched down" twice to release the extra gas.

Wholesome Waffles with Strawberry Compote (page 32)

CHAPTER 3

BREAKFAST TREATS

love breakfast. It is my favorite meal of the day, and from the moment my eyes open, I can't wait for morning nourishment to brighten my day. These breakfast treats will fuel you with the right nutrients, including filling fiber, energizing carbs, and muscle-building proteins. Make a few extra servings of pancakes, waffles, and muffins such as Blueberry-Lemon Muffins or hearty Chai Spiced Multigrain Oatmeal Muffins on the weekends to have on hand for busy weekday mornings. Whether you are in the mood for something warm on a cold winter day or in need of a grab-and-go meal while running out the door, here are 11 offerings to start your day in a cheery, happy mood.

Triple Berry Baked Oatmeal

CONTAINS COCONUT | SOY-FREE

Prepping baked oatmeal the night before makes mornings much more manageable. Bursting with berry flavor and a hint of orange and cinnamon, this meal makes a perfect summer dish. Change it up for fall and winter by substituting apples or pears for the berries.
To add a sweet topping, dollop with a scoop of dairy-free yogurt. This is best served immediately.

PREP TIME: 15 MINUTES
BAKE TIME: 35 MINUTES
SERVES 12

2 cups certified gluten-free rolled oats

3 tablespoons light brown sugar or coconut sugar

2 tablespoons chia seeds

1 teaspoon baking powder

1 teaspoon ground cinnamon

¼ teaspoon salt

1¾ cups unsweetened dairy-free milk

⅓ cup maple syrup

¼ cup freshly squeezed orange juice

2 large eggs

2 teaspoons vanilla extract

1½ tablespoons coconut oil, melted

1 cup diced, hulled strawberries

½ cup blueberries

½ cup raspberries

1. Preheat the oven to 375°F. Lightly coat a 9-by-13-inch baking dish with nonstick cooking spray.

2. In a large bowl, combine the oats, sugar, chia seeds, baking powder, cinnamon, and salt. Mix well.

3. In a medium bowl, whisk together the milk, maple syrup, orange juice, eggs, and vanilla. Add the milk mixture and oil to the oat mixture. Stir until well blended.

4. Sprinkle the strawberries in the bottom of the prepared dish. Add the oat mixture in an even layer. Sprinkle with the blueberries and raspberries. Cover the dish with aluminum foil.

5. Bake until a knife inserted in the center comes out clean, 30 to 35 minutes. Serve warm.

PREP TIP: If using frozen berries, thaw and drain them prior to adding them to the dish.

Wholesome Waffles with Strawberry Compote

NUT-FREE | SOY-FREE

One of our family's favorite traditions is to make waffles and pancakes on the weekends. My kids drown their
waffles in maple syrup, while my husband and I love
them with this strawberry compote. For a new dessert
idea, enjoy the compote over dairy-free ice cream.

PREP TIME: **15 MINUTES**
BAKE TIME: **20 MINUTES**
SERVES 6

For the strawberry compote

**1 pint (16 ounces) strawberries,
hulled and diced**

¼ cup water

**2 tablespoons honey or
maple syrup**

**1 teaspoon freshly squeezed
lemon juice**

For the waffles

**2 cups plus 1 tablespoon Basic
Gluten-Free Flour Blend (page 10)
or store-bought equivalent**

1 tablespoon baking powder

½ teaspoon salt

**1½ cups unsweetened dairy-
free milk**

6 tablespoons vegan butter, melted

¼ cup maple syrup

1 tablespoon vanilla extract

2 large eggs, separated

2 large egg whites

1. For the strawberry compote, in a small
saucepan, combine the strawberries, water, and
honey. Bring to a simmer over medium heat
and cook until the mixture thickens, about
7 minutes. Stir in the lemon juice and transfer
to a bowl. Let cool slightly.

2. For the waffles, lightly coat a waffle iron
with nonstick cooking spray. Preheat the iron
according to the manufacturer's directions.

3. In a large bowl, combine the flour blend,
baking powder, and salt.

4. In a medium bowl, whisk together the milk,
butter, maple syrup, vanilla, and egg yolks. Stir
into the flour mixture just until blended. Be
careful not to overmix.

5. In a large bowl, using an electric mixer on
high speed, beat the egg whites until soft peaks
form. Fold into the batter, one-third at a time,
just until blended.

6. Pour ½ cup of the batter (or according to the
manufacturer's directions) onto the hot waffle
iron. Cook until golden brown and crisp. Serve
hot with the strawberry compote.

PREP TIP: Make sure to beat the egg whites to soft peaks rather than stiff to create a light and fluffy waffle.

STORAGE: These waffles do not last long in our home! If they do in yours, store in an airtight container in the refrigerator for up to 1 week.

SUBSTITUTIONS: You can substitute equal amounts of any fruit such as blueberries, raspberries, blackberries, or diced peaches for the strawberries in the compote.

Silver Dollar Pancakes

NUT-FREE | SOY-FREE

These simple, fluffy pancakes are sure to be a crowd-pleaser. Serve them drizzled with maple syrup or honey or topped with dairy-free vanilla yogurt and chopped nuts. My kids love them sandwiched with nut butter for a handheld meal. These store beautifully, so don't be afraid to double the batch!

PREP TIME: 15 MINUTES
BAKE TIME: 20 MINUTES
SERVES 4

1 cup Basic Gluten-Free Flour Blend (page 10) or store-bought equivalent

2½ teaspoons baking powder

¼ teaspoon salt

2 large eggs

1 cup unsweetened dairy-free milk

3 tablespoons extra-virgin olive oil or avocado oil

2 tablespoons maple syrup

1 tablespoon white vinegar

1. Lightly coat a griddle with nonstick cooking spray. Heat over medium heat.

2. In a large bowl, combine the flour blend, baking powder, and salt.

3. In a small bowl, whisk together the eggs, milk, oil, maple syrup, and vinegar. Pour over the flour mixture and stir just until combined. Let stand for 5 minutes. The batter may be slightly lumpy.

4. Lower the heat to medium low. Drop a scant ¼ cup of batter onto the griddle. Cook until bubbles form, 2 to 3 minutes. Flip and cook until golden brown, another 2 minutes. Repeat this process with the remaining batter. Serve warm.

STORAGE: Store in the refrigerator in an airtight container for up to 5 days, or freeze in a zip-top plastic bag for up to 1 month.

Pecan-Crusted Sweet Potato Breakfast Bake

CONTAINS COCONUT | SOY-FREE

Sweet potato, pecans, and warm spices form this delicious breakfast dish that's a cross between a quiche and a cake. A warm slice of this with a cup of coffee or tea is all you need for a hearty breakfast. This bake can also be served as a side at any holiday feast.

PREP TIME: 15 MINUTES, PLUS SWEET POTATO COOK TIME

BAKE TIME: 30 MINUTES

SERVES 4 TO 6

Coconut oil, for coating

1 large sweet potato, cooked, peeled, and mashed (see prep tip)

1 cup unsweetened applesauce

1 large carrot, chopped (¾ cup)

4 large eggs

½ cup plain dairy-free yogurt

1 teaspoon vanilla extract

1 teaspoon ground cinnamon

½ teaspoon ground ginger

½ teaspoon ground nutmeg

½ teaspoon salt

1½ cups chopped pecans

1. Preheat the oven to 400°F. Lightly coat a 9-inch cast iron skillet with coconut oil.

2. In a blender, put the sweet potato, applesauce, carrots, eggs, yogurt, vanilla, cinnamon, ginger, nutmeg, and salt. Blend until combined and smooth.

3. Pour the mixture into the prepared skillet. Top with the pecans. Bake until a knife inserted in the center comes out clean, about 30 minutes.

PREP TIP: Leftover baked sweet potatoes are convenient for this recipe, but if you don't have any on hand, pierce a large sweet potato several times with a fork. Preheat the oven to 400°F and bake until tender, 1 to 1½ hours. Or, to prep in the microwave, cook on high until tender, 5 to 10 minutes. When the potato has cooled, remove the skin. It should make about 2 cups.

STORAGE: This is best served warm from the oven, but to save for another day, store in an airtight container in the refrigerator for up to 5 days.

VARIATION: If you prefer a little more texture, don't add the carrots to the blender. Instead, stir them into the batter. If you are feeling extravagant, use the scraped seeds of a vanilla bean instead of the vanilla extract.

Blueberry-Lemon Muffins

SOY-FREE

The classic flavor combination of lemon and blueberries in these incredibly moist and tasty muffins is a perfect way to start your day. For larger muffins, divide the batter among 12 muffin cups and bake for 3 to 5 minutes longer.

PREP TIME: 15 MINUTES
BAKE TIME: 30 MINUTES
MAKES 17 MUFFINS

2 large egg whites

1 large egg

1¾ cups plain dairy-free yogurt

½ cup maple syrup

½ cup granulated sugar

Grated zest from 2 large lemons (2 teaspoons)

2 teaspoons freshly squeezed lemon juice

1½ cups Basic Gluten-Free Flour Blend (page 10) or store-bought equivalent

1 cup almond meal

1 teaspoon baking powder

½ teaspoon baking soda

½ teaspoon salt

1 cup blueberries

1. Preheat the oven to 350°F. Line two 12-cup muffin pans with 17 cupcake liners. Lightly coat each liner with nonstick cooking spray.

2. In a large bowl, whisk together the egg whites, egg, yogurt, maple syrup, sugar, lemon zest, and lemon juice. Add the flour blend, almond meal, baking powder, baking soda, and salt. Stir just until combined, then carefully fold in the blueberries.

3. Divide among the prepared muffin cups. Bake until the tops are slightly browned and a toothpick inserted in the center comes out clean, about 30 minutes. Let cool for 10 minutes, then transfer to a wire rack to cool completely.

PREP TIP: You can also make this recipe into a quick bread. Pour the batter into a 9-inch loaf pan lined with parchment paper and lightly coated with nonstick cooking spray. Bake for 50 to 60 minutes.

STORAGE: Store at room temperature in an airtight container for up to 3 days, or freeze in a zip-top plastic bag up to 3 months.

Chai-Spiced Multigrain Oatmeal Muffins

CONTAINS COCONUT | SOY-FREE

Looking to get a good serving of fiber in the morning? These hearty breakfast muffins provide fiber to keep you full longer and help reduce cholesterol.

PREP TIME: 15 MINUTES
BAKE TIME: 25 MINUTES
MAKES 12 MUFFINS

2 large eggs

½ cup vanilla dairy-free yogurt

½ cup maple syrup

1 teaspoon vanilla extract

1 cup Gluten-Free Whole-Grain Flour Blend (page 11) or store-bought equivalent

1 cup certified gluten-free quick-cooking oats

¼ cup flaxseed meal

2 teaspoons baking powder

1 teaspoon ground cinnamon

½ teaspoon ground ginger

½ teaspoon ground nutmeg

½ teaspoon baking soda

½ teaspoon salt

½ cup coconut oil, melted

1. Preheat the oven to 350°F. Lightly coat a 12-cup muffin pan with nonstick cooking spray.

2. In a small bowl, whisk together the eggs, yogurt, maple syrup, and vanilla.

3. In a large bowl, stir together the flour blend, oats, flaxseed meal, baking powder, cinnamon, ginger, nutmeg, baking soda, and salt. Stir in the egg mixture and the coconut oil just until combined.

4. Divide among the prepared muffin cups. Bake until the tops are slightly browned and a toothpick inserted in the center comes out clean, 18 to 22 minutes. Let cool for 10 minutes, then transfer to a wire rack to cool completely.

PREP TIP: Make sure to use quick-cooking oats, as rolled oats will absorb too much moisture, resulting in a dry muffin.

STORAGE: Store at room temperature in an airtight container for up to 3 days, or freeze in a zip-top plastic bag up to 3 months.

Banana-Zucchini Muffins

NUT-FREE | SOY-FREE

The key to these moist banana-zucchini muffins is the bananas and fresh zucchini. They are one of my favorite ways to get vegetables and fruit in my boys first thing in the morning! To entice picky children, stir ½ cup of dairy-free mini chocolate chips into the batter with the zucchini mixture.

PREP TIME: 15 MINUTES
BAKE TIME: 25 MINUTES
MAKES 12 MUFFINS

1½ cup Basic Gluten-Free Flour Blend (page 10) or store-bought equivalent

¾ cup packed light brown sugar or coconut sugar

2 teaspoons baking powder

1 teaspoon ground cinnamon

½ teaspoon baking soda

½ teaspoon salt

1 small zucchini, chopped (about 1 cup)

1 small banana, peeled

½ cup unsweetened applesauce

2 large eggs

1 teaspoon vanilla extract

1. Preheat the oven to 350°F. Line a 12-cup muffin pan with cupcake liners. Lightly coat each liner with nonstick cooking spray.

2. In a large bowl, whisk together the flour blend, sugar, baking powder, cinnamon, baking soda, and salt.

3. In a blender, put the zucchini, banana, applesauce, eggs, and vanilla. Blend until very smooth. Stir into the flour mixture just until combined.

4. Divide among the prepared muffin cups. Bake until the tops are slightly browned and a toothpick inserted in the center comes out clean, 18 to 22 minutes. Let cool for 10 minutes, then transfer to a wire rack to cool completely.

REHEATING TIP: If not eating right away, these muffins are best reheated after storage. Place on a small plate and microwave for 5 to 10 seconds.

STORAGE: Store at room temperature in an airtight container for up to 3 days, or freeze in a zip-top plastic bag up to 3 months.

Cinnamon-Maple Scones with Maple Glaze

SOY-FREE

I never thought I would taste such delicate scones that were gluten-free. The combination of yogurt and vegan butter makes these scones a light, fluffy, and healthy choice that still bursts with classic, delicious flavor.

PREP TIME: **15 MINUTES**
BAKE TIME: **20 MINUTES**
MAKES 8 SCONES

1 large egg
1 large egg white
½ cup plain dairy-free yogurt
⅓ cup maple syrup
3 teaspoons maple extract, divided
2 cups Gluten-Free Cake and Pastry Flour Blend (page 11) or store-bought equivalent
½ cup tapioca flour
1 tablespoon baking powder
2 teaspoons ground cinnamon
½ teaspoon baking soda
½ teaspoon salt
½ cup chilled vegan butter
1 cup confectioners' sugar
1 tablespoon unsweetened dairy-free milk
Light brown sugar or coconut sugar, for sprinkling (optional)

STORAGE: Store at room temperature in an airtight container for up to 3 days, or freeze in a zip-top plastic bag lined with paper towels on top and bottom for up to 3 months.

1. Preheat the oven to 400°F. Line a baking sheet with parchment paper or a silicone baking mat.

2. In a large bowl, combine the egg, egg white, yogurt, maple syrup, and 2 teaspoons of maple extract. Whisk together until smooth and creamy.

3. Add the flour blend, tapioca flour, baking powder, cinnamon, baking soda, and salt. Using a pastry blender or two knives, cut in the butter until it forms crumbs. Stir in the egg mixture until well blended and using your hands to knead the dough if necessary. Add a sprinkle of the flour blend if too sticky.

4. Form the dough into a ball and place on the prepared baking sheet. With floured hands, press to an 8-inch disk. Using a chef knife, slice the dough into 8 wedges. Using a metal spatula, gently pull the scones 2 inches apart. Bake until golden brown, about 17 minutes. Let cool for 5 minutes, then transfer to a wire rack to cool completely.

5. In a small bowl, whisk together confectioners' sugar, milk, and the remaining 1 teaspoon of maple extract. Pour over the scones and top each with a sprinkle of brown sugar (if using).

Lazy Day Cinnamon Coffee Cake

SOY-FREE

This cake is my husband's favorite, and one he requests often! To easily remove the cake from the pan, I like to cut the parchment paper to fit the bottom and two sides of the pan with a 2-inch overhang on each side. The overhang makes handles for lifting out the cake.

PREP TIME: **15 MINUTES**
BAKE TIME: **50 MINUTES**
SERVES **16**

1¾ cups packed light brown sugar or coconut sugar, divided

1 cup chopped walnuts

1 tablespoon ground cinnamon

2¼ cups Gluten-Free Cake and Pastry Flour Blend (page 11) or store-bought equivalent

1 tablespoon baking powder

1 teaspoon baking soda

½ teaspoon salt

½ cup vegan butter, at room temperature

2 large eggs

1 cup vanilla dairy-free yogurt

2½ teaspoons vanilla extract

STORAGE: Store in an airtight container at room temperature for up to 3 days or in the refrigerator for up to 5 days. Best served warm.

SUBSTITUTIONS: You can substitute pecans for the walnuts or leave the nuts out altogether.

1. Preheat the oven to 350°F. Line a 9-inch square baking pan with parchment paper.

2. In a small bowl, stir together ¾ cup of sugar, the walnuts, and the cinnamon. Set aside.

3. In a medium bowl, combine the flour blend, baking powder, baking soda, and salt.

4. In a large bowl, using an electric mixer on high speed, beat the butter and the remaining 1 cup of sugar together until light and fluffy. Add the eggs, yogurt, and vanilla and beat just until blended. Slowly add the flour mixture, one-third at a time, mixing until well blended.

5. Spoon half the batter into the prepared pan. Evenly sprinkle with half the nut mixture. Spoon the remaining batter over the walnuts to cover completely, then sprinkle with the remaining nut mixture. Bake until a toothpick inserted in the center comes out clean, 45 to 50 minutes.

6. Let cool for 10 minutes, then transfer to a wire rack to cool completely.

Oaty Peanut Butter Breakfast Cookies

CONTAINS COCONUT | SOY-FREE

These incredibly moist cookies are packed with fiber, whole grains, protein, and fruit. Keep them on hand for a grab-and-go breakfast for busy mornings. They also make a great afternoon pick-me-up.

PREP TIME: **15 MINUTES**
BAKE TIME: **15 MINUTES**
MAKES 24 COOKIES

3 ripe bananas

1 large egg, beaten

½ cup natural peanut butter

3 tablespoons maple syrup

1 tablespoon coconut oil, melted

1 tablespoon chia seeds

1½ teaspoons vanilla extract

2½ cups certified gluten-free rolled oats

1 teaspoon baking powder

¼ teaspoon salt

½ cup dairy-free mini chocolate chips or ½ cup dried cranberries

½ cup pumpkin seeds (optional)

1. Preheat the oven to 350°F. Line two baking sheets with parchment paper or silicone baking mats.

2. In a large bowl, mash the bananas with a fork until smooth. Stir in the egg, peanut butter, maple syrup, coconut oil, chia seeds, and vanilla until blended. Add the oats, baking powder, and salt and stir until combined. Stir in the chocolate chips and pumpkin seeds (if using).

3. With a 2-inch cookie scoop, divide the dough into 24 scoops, and arrange 12 per pan, 2 inches apart. With a glass, flatten the dough. Bake until they are slightly browned, about 15 minutes. Let cool for 10 minutes, then transfer to a wire rack to cool completely.

STORAGE: Store at room temperature in an airtight container for up to 3 days.

SUBSTITUTIONS: Substitute any nut or seed butter, such as almond or sunflower seed, for the peanut butter. Note that sunflower seed butter may turn the cookies slightly green, which is natural and safe.

Biscuits

NUT-FREE | SOY-FREE

Biscuits are an American favorite and something many gluten-free people think they have to give up. You can enjoy these tender biscuits many ways, such as smothered in gravy, spread with butter and jam, or as a side for holiday feasts and brunches. My family loves them as the bread for ham sandwiches or the base for strawberry shortcakes with coconut whipped cream (see page 122).

PREP TIME: 15 MINUTES
BAKE TIME: 15 MINUTES
MAKES 8 BISCUITS

2 cups Basic Gluten-Free Flour Blend (page 10) or store-bought equivalent

1½ tablespoons baking powder

½ teaspoon salt

½ cup vegan butter, cold

1 large egg, beaten

⅔ cup unsweetened dairy-free milk

1 tablespoon maple syrup

2 teaspoons apple cider vinegar

PREP TiP: If you'd like, brush the biscuits will some extra melted butter before baking. These biscuits are best served warm. Serve them immediately, or reheat in the microwave on high for 5 to 10 seconds before serving.

STORAGE: Store at room temperature in an airtight container for up to 2 days.

1. Preheat the oven to 450°F. Line a baking sheet with parchment paper or a silicone baking mat.

2. In a large bowl, combine the flour blend, baking powder, and salt. Cut in the butter with a fork or two knives until it forms crumbs. Stir in the egg, milk, maple syrup, and vinegar. Mix to form a dough.

3. Transfer dough to a lightly floured work surface. With lightly floured hands, shape into a ball and flatten to ¾-inch thickness. Using a biscuit cutter, cut the dough into rounds and place on the prepared baking sheet. Reshape the scraps of dough and repeat cutting out the dough to make eight biscuits.

4. Bake until golden brown, about 12 minutes. Let cool for 5 minutes, then transfer to a wire rack to cool completely. Serve warm.

Olive and Herb Focaccia Bread (page 53)

CHAPTER
4

YEAST BREADS AND ROLLS

45

you may have shopped for gluten-free bread, only to find it is limited in variety, very expensive, comes in smaller than typical slices, and usually crumbles apart unless toasted. Not to mention, it contains unnecessary preservatives. Homemade gluten-free breads, on the other hand, are not only safe from gluten contamination but also contain more nutritional value from the inclusion of whole grains and natural sugars. The basic white and multigrain bread loaves are essentials for everyday eating, best used for sandwiches and toast. Try sourdough, warm from the oven, with a steaming bowl of soup or along with a salad, or delicious focaccia, which is a fabulous addition to Italian night.

White Bread Loaf

NUT-FREE | SOY-FREE

Nothing compares to a home filled with the aroma of freshly baked bread! Although you'll want to start slicing into it right out of the oven, this bread slices best the day after baking.

PREP TIME: **30 MINUTES, PLUS 3 HOURS TO RISE**

BAKE TIME: **1 HOUR**

MAKES 1 LOAF

2¼ teaspoons instant rise yeast

2 tablespoons sugar

½ cup lukewarm water

4 large eggs

¼ cup extra virgin olive oil

1 teaspoon apple cider vinegar

2¼ cups sweet white rice flour

½ cup tapioca flour

1 cup cornstarch

½ cup egg white powder

1 tablespoon xanthan gum

1 tablespoon baking powder

1 teaspoon salt

1¼ cups unsweetened dairy-free milk

1. In a small bowl, dissolve the yeast and 1 tablespoon of sugar in the water. Stir with a fork until the yeast dissolves, and let stand until the yeast foams and is activated, 5 to 10 minutes.

2. In a small bowl, combine the eggs, oil, vinegar, and the remaining 1 tablespoon of sugar and mix well.

3. In a large bowl, stir together the flours, cornstarch, egg white powder, xanthan gum, baking powder, and salt. Add the egg mixture, yeast mixture, and dairy-free milk. Stir, continually folding with a spatula, until fully combined, 5 to 8 minutes. The mixture will be slightly watery and sticky at this point.

4. Line the bottom and sides of a 9-inch loaf pan with parchment paper so there is an overhang on two sides. Transfer the dough to the pan. Cover with plastic wrap and set in a warm, draft-free place to rise for 3 hours.

5. After 3 hours, preheat the oven to 350°F.

6. Bake until the top is browned, about 1 hour. Let cool for 10 minutes, then remove from the pan by lifting the parchment paper. Transfer to a wire rack to cool completely.

CONTINUED

White Bread Loaf CONTINUED

BREAD MACHINE INSTRUCTIONS: Put all the wet ingredients in the machine first, then add the dry ingredients. Make a well in the dry ingredients and add the yeast, making sure it does not touch the liquid. Start the bread machine according to the manufacturer's instructions.

STORAGE: Make sure the bread has cooled completely before storing. Line aluminum foil with wax paper. Wrap the loaf tightly, then transfer to a zip-top plastic bag. The bread keeps best in the refrigerator for about 1 week. To freeze, slice the bread, then wrap it in the same way and freeze for up to 3 months.

BREAD MACHINES

Growing up, my mom always used her bread machine to make homemade bread. She would then slice the loaf into large Texas-size slices and make French toast for us on the weekends. I still remember the sweet aromas of freshly baked bread filling up every room in the house. I felt her love, nourishment, and care for me—ironically, through bread.

Investing in a good bread machine will save you so much time when making homemade breads, rolls, and pizza crusts. I love my Zojirushi model, taking on my mother's tradition and using it every week. We bake fresh loaves, or I set it to blend the dough for family Friday night pizza.

There are many more brands that can be found online, such as Oster, SKG, Panasonic, Sunbeam, Breadman, Hamilton Beach, and Cuisinart.

Multigrain Bread Loaf

NUT-FREE | SOY-FREE

My love for fresh homemade breads started when I was 12 and my mother baked a loaf every week. Today, I carry on the tradition in our home. This version uses multigrain flour for extra fiber. It is perfect for sandwiches and toast, and slices best the day after baking.

PREP TIME: 30 MINUTES, PLUS 3 HOURS TO RISE

BAKE TIME: 1 HOUR

MAKES 1 LOAF

2¼ teaspoons instant rise yeast

3 tablespoons honey or maple syrup, divided

1⅓ cups lukewarm water

4 large eggs

3 tablespoons extra-virgin olive oil

2 teaspoons apple cider vinegar

2 cups Gluten-Free Whole-Grain Flour Blend (page 11) or store-bought equivalent

⅔ cup coconut milk powder, egg white powder, or almond meal

½ cup tapioca flour

½ cup potato starch

⅓ cup arrowroot

1 tablespoon xanthan gum

1½ teaspoons salt

1. In a small bowl, dissolve the yeast and 1 tablespoon of honey in the water. Stir with a fork until the yeast dissolves, and let stand until the yeast foams and is activated, 5 to 10 minutes.

2. In a small bowl, combine the eggs, oil, vinegar, and the remaining 2 tablespoons of honey and mix well.

3. In a large bowl, mix together the flour blend, milk powder, tapioca flour, potato starch, arrowroot, xanthan gum, and salt. Add the egg mixture and yeast mixture. Stir, continually folding with a spatula, until fully combined, 5 to 8 minutes. The mixture will be slightly watery and sticky at this point.

4. Cover the bowl with plastic wrap and set in a warm, draft-free place to rise for 3 hours.

5. After 3 hours, preheat the oven to 350°F. Line a 9-inch loaf pan with parchment paper so there is an overhang on two sides.

6. Transfer the dough with a rubber spatula to the prepared pan (it is still sticky at this point). Bake until the top is browned, about 1 hour. Let cool for 10 minutes, then remove by lifting the parchment paper. Transfer to a wire rack to cool completely.

CONTINUED

BREAD MACHINE INSTRUCTIONS: Put all the wet ingredients in the machine first, then add the dry ingredients. Make a well in the dry ingredients and add the yeast, making sure it does not touch the liquid. Start the bread machine according to the manufacturer's instructions.

STORAGE: Make sure the bread has cooled completely before storing. Line aluminum foil with wax paper. Wrap the loaf tightly, then transfer to a zip-top plastic bag. The bread keeps best in the refrigerator for about 1 week. To freeze, slice the bread, then wrap it in the same way and freeze for up to 3 months.

BREAD DOUGH MAKING TIPS

* Make sure the temperature of the liquid you add to the yeast is between 110°F and 120°F, otherwise it can negatively affect the yeast (or even kill it). If the yeast is still not foaming, try adding a teaspoon of sweetener, such as sugar or honey, to give it some fuel and hopefully jump-start fermentation and increase your rise.

* Gluten-free bread dough rises best when resting in a warm, draft-free place with lots of moisture.

* The dough should be moist and sticky with a light texture, rather than dense and heavy. It is best to let the dough rise at this point and add more flour after rising.

* Adding dairy-free milk to baked goods such as focaccia and loaf breads yields a delicious, moist, and chewy bread. If your final result seems too moist, try baking it longer or adding less liquid the next time.

Sourdough Bread

NUT-FREE | SOY-FREE | VEGAN

This gorgeous rustic bread with a crispy exterior and soft center is baked in a Dutch oven and is so delicious you will savor every bite. But good things come to those who wait, because this loaf takes about 7 days to prepare. You may want to begin the starter on the weekend (it just needs to be stirred twice a day during the week) and finish the baking on the following weekend.

PREP TIME: 1 HOUR, PLUS 12 HOURS TO RISE AND 6 DAYS TO MAKE THE STARTER
BAKE TIME: 1 HOUR
MAKES 1 LOAF

For the sourdough starter
1 tablespoon granulated sugar
3 cups water, divided
3 cups brown rice flour, divided

For the bread
1 cup Basic Gluten Free Flour Blend (page 10) or store-bought equivalent
½ cup garbanzo bean flour
½ cup arrowroot
¼ cup potato starch
¼ cup psyllium husk
1 teaspoon xanthan gum
1 tablespoon salt
3 tablespoons extra-virgin olive oil
1 tablespoon maple syrup
1½ cups water

1. For the sourdough starter, in a glass bowl, whisk together the sugar, ¼ cup of water, and ¼ cup of brown rice flour briskly for 30 seconds to aerate. Cover with a dish towel and let stand on the kitchen counter away from direct sunlight. Twice a day, morning and night, discard about 1 tablespoon of the mixture, then add ¼ cup of brown rice flour and ¼ cup of water to feed the starter. Beat briskly with a whisk each time to aerate. Continue for 6 days until you start to see bubbles appear on the surface and it starts to rise.

2. For the bread, in a large bowl, combine the flour blend, garbanzo bean flour, arrowroot, potato starch, psyllium husk, xanthan gum, and salt. Make a well in the center and add the oil, maple syrup, water, and 2 cups of sourdough starter. Stir vigorously for 10 minutes (this can be done with an electric mixer using a dough hook) to combine and aerate into the batter. The consistency will be sticky and wet. Cover with a dish towel or plastic wrap, and leave in a warm place to rise for 12 hours or overnight.

3. Preheat the oven to 450°F.

CONTINUED

4. Place the dough on a sheet of parchment paper and form it into a ball. If needed, add a sprinkle of flour, just enough to handle. Using a knife, cut two slits forming an "X" about ¼ inch into the dough. Let the dough rest for 25 minutes.

5. While the dough rests, place a Dutch oven on a pizza stone in the oven and let it preheat for 25 minutes.

6. When the Dutch oven is heated, transfer the parchment paper with the dough into the Dutch oven. Cover and bake for 25 minutes. Remove the lid and bake for another 25 minutes.

7. Remove the Dutch oven from the oven and place the bread directly on the pizza stone. Bake until the bread is golden brown and sounds hollow when tapped, another 8 to 10 minutes. Let cool for 10 minutes, then transfer to a wire rack to cool completely.

PREP TIP: The first time you make this, test the center for doneness. If the bread is underbaked and too moist in the center, return it to the Dutch oven and the oven. If you are not sure if it's done, cut into the loaf with a knife. Let it stand in the warm oven (with the oven turned off), and check every 10 minutes until the center is no longer moist. Note the baking time for future loaves.

STORAGE: Make sure the bread has cooled completely before storing. Store at room temperature in an airtight container for up to 3 days.

Olive and Herb Focaccia Bread

NUT-FREE | SOY-FREE

This focaccia bread is loaded with heart-healthy olive oil, which may seem like too much, but it is what makes the crust extra-flavorful.

PREP TIME: 40 MINUTES, PLUS 1 HOUR AND 45 MINUTES TO RISE
BAKE TIME: 25 MINUTES
SERVES 8

Extra-virgin olive oil, for greasing

4½ teaspoons instant rise yeast

1 cup lukewarm water

4½ cups Basic Gluten-Free Flour Blend (page 10) or store-bought equivalent

1½ tablespoons xanthan gum

2 teaspoons salt

4 large eggs

1 cup unsweetened dairy-free milk

¾ cup extra-virgin olive oil, divided

2 teaspoons apple cider vinegar

24 green or black olives, pitted and chopped

2 teaspoons chopped fresh rosemary

2 teaspoons chopped fresh thyme

Grated zest of 1 large lemon (1 teaspoon; see step 8 before grating)

Kosher salt (optional)

1. Grease a large bowl with oil. Line a 12-by-18-inch baking pan with parchment paper.

2. In a small bowl, dissolve the yeast in the water. Stir with a fork until the yeast dissolved and let stand until the yeast foams and is activated, 5 to 10 minutes.

3. In a large bowl, combine the flour blend, xanthan gum, and salt.

4. In a medium bowl, whisk together the eggs, milk, 2 tablespoons of oil, and the vinegar. Stir into the flour mixture.

5. When the yeast is activated, stir it into the flour mixture. Continue to "knead" with a spatula for about 10 minutes. The dough will be sticky.

6. Place the dough in the prepared bowl, turning to coat. Cover with plastic wrap and set in a warm, draft-free place to rise until doubled in size, about 1½ hours.

7. Pour 5 tablespoons of oil in the prepared pan. Add the dough (it will still be very sticky) to the center of the pan. If needed, sprinkle with flour to handle the dough. Using your fingertips, press out the dough into a 13-by-10-inch rectangle. Let rest for 10 minutes.

CONTINUED

8. Sprinkle the olives, rosemary, and thyme on top of the dough. Grate the lemon zest directly over the dough. Pour the remaining 5 table-spoons of oil evenly over the top. Cover with plastic wrap and let rise for 25 minutes.

9. Preheat the oven to 475°F.

10. When dough is ready, press with fingertips all over to form indentions. Bake until the top is golden brown and the edges are crusty, 20 to 25 minutes. Sprinkle with kosher salt (if using), cut into pieces, and serve.

STORAGE: Store in a zip-top plastic bag at room temperature for up to 3 days or in the refrigerator for up to 1 week. Reheat in the microwave for 10 seconds.

SUBSTITUTIONS: You can swap out the rosemary and thyme for basil and oregano.

Cardamom Sweet Bread

NUT-FREE | SOY-FREE

The moments waiting for this bread to bake never seem short enough. Enjoy it spread with dairy-free butter mixed with a drop of honey.

PREP TIME: **1 HOUR, PLUS 2 HOURS TO RISE**
BAKE TIME: **1 HOUR**
MAKES 1 LOAF

2¼ teaspoons instant rise yeast
½ cup granulated sugar, divided
½ cup lukewarm water
1 cup unsweetened dairy-free milk, scalded (see prep tip, page 56)
½ cup vegan butter
1 teaspoon salt
4 large eggs
2 cups sweet white rice flour
1 cup cornstarch
½ cup egg white powder
½ cup tapioca flour
1 tablespoon xanthan gum
1 tablespoon baking powder
2 teaspoons ground cardamom

1. Line a 9-inch loaf pan with parchment paper so there is an overhand on two sides. Set aside.

2. In a large bowl, dissolve the yeast and ½ teaspoon of sugar in the water. Stir with a fork until the yeast dissolves and let stand until the yeast foams and is activated, 5 to 10 minutes.

3. To the scalded milk, add the butter, the remaining sugar, and salt and stir until the sugar is dissolved. Let cool to lukewarm.

4. Add the milk mixture to the yeast, then add the eggs, sweet white rice flour, cornstarch, egg white powder, tapioca flour, xanthan gum, baking powder, and cardamom, and mix just until a dough forms.

5. Form the dough into a ball and put in the prepared baking pan to rise. Spread it out easily. Cover with plastic wrap and set in a warm, draft-free place to rise until doubled in size, about 2 hours.

6. Preheat the oven 350°F. Line a 9-inch loaf pan with parchment paper so there is an overhang on two sides.

7. Bake until golden brown, about 1 hour. Let cool for 10 minutes, then remove from the pan by lifting the parchment paper. Transfer to a wire rack to cool completely.

CONTINUED

Cardamom Sweet Bread CONTINUED

PREP TIP: Adding scalded milk to yeast breads helps get a better rise from the yeast. To scald the milk, heat a small saucepan over medium-high heat and add the milk. Cook until the milk bubbles slightly around the edges but does not boil, until it reaches 180°F. As soon as the edges start to bubble, remove from the heat.

STORAGE: Make sure the bread has cooled completely before storing. Line aluminum foil with wax paper. Wrap the loaf tightly, then transfer to a zip-top plastic bag. The bread keeps best in the refrigerator for about 1 week. To freeze, slice the bread, then wrap it in the same way and freeze for up to 3 months.

VARIATIONS: Turn this into cinnamon bread by replacing the cardamom with ground cinnamon, or use ground allspice and a pinch of nutmeg for a harvest bread.

Bagels

NUT-FREE | SOY-FREE

Fluffy bagels are a staple breakfast item for busy mornings, and in my home, they are best served with dairy-free cream cheese or homemade jam. You can also keep them on hand to use throughout the week for sandwiches.

PREP TIME: **1 HOUR, PLUS 1 HOUR AND 30 MINUTES TO RISE**
BAKE TIME: **35 MINUTES**
MAKES 12 BAGELS

4½ teaspoon instant rise yeast
2 tablespoons maple syrup
1 cup lukewarm water
4½ cups Basic Gluten-Free Flour Blend (page 10) or store-bought equivalent
1½ tablespoons xanthan gum
1 tablespoon baking powder
2 teaspoons salt
4 large eggs
1 cup unsweetened dairy-free milk
¼ cup extra-virgin olive oil
2 teaspoons apple cider vinegar
Dried onion flakes, sesame seeds, poppy seeds, or everything bagel seasoning (optional)

1. Line a baking sheet with parchment paper.

2. In a small bowl, dissolve the yeast and maple syrup in the water. Stir with a fork until the yeast dissolves, and let stand until the yeast foams and is activated, 5 to 10 minutes.

3. In a medium bowl, whisk together the flour blend, xanthan gum, baking powder, and salt. In a large bowl, using an electric mixer on low speed, beat together the eggs, milk, olive oil, and vinegar until blended. Add the dry mixture and mix just until a moist dough forms, about 3 minutes.

4. Place the dough on a floured work surface and divide into 12 balls. Flour your hands, then roll the balls into 7-inch-long ropes and form each one into a bagel, wetting the ends, then pressing them together to seal. Place on the prepared baking sheet and cover with plastic wrap. Set in a warm, draft-free place to rise for 1½ hours.

5. Preheat the oven 400°F.

6. Fill a large saucepan with 4 inches of water and bring to a boil over high heat. Add the bagels, two to four at a time, to the boiling water

CONTINUED

Bagels CONTINUED

and cook for 3 minutes, turning once half-way through the cooking time. Remove from the water with a slotted spatula or spoon and return to the same baking sheet. Repeat with the remaining dough.

7. Brush the bagels with the remaining 1 tablespoon of oil. Sprinkle with onion flakes (if using).

8. Bake until the tops and sides are slightly brown, 20 to 25 minutes. Let cool for 5 minutes, then transfer to a wire rack to cool completely.

PREP TIP: When you form the dough into bagel shapes, make sure the ends are sealed together well so they do not fall apart when boiling.

STORAGE: Store at room temperature in an airtight container for up to 2 days.

Homemade Dinner Rolls

NUT-FREE | SOY-FREE

Serve these rolls at your next dinner party when you crave a little extra comfort food. Or use them to make melty mini cold-cut sandwiches. Slice the rolls and layer with the cold cuts of your choice. Top with vegan cheese and place in a baking dish. Bake at 350°F for 10 minutes or until the cheese melts.

PREP TIME: 35 MINUTES, PLUS 4 HOURS AND 30 MINUTES TO RISE
BAKE TIME: 20 MINUTES
MAKES 12 ROLLS

4½ teaspoons instant rise yeast

1 cup lukewarm water

2 tablespoons maple syrup

4½ cups Basic Gluten-Free Flour Blend (page 10) or store-bought equivalent

1 tablespoon baking powder

1½ tablespoons xanthan gum

2 teaspoons salt

4 large eggs

1 cup unsweetened dairy-free milk

¼ cup extra-virgin olive oil

2 teaspoons apple cider vinegar

2 tablespoons warm water or 1 egg yolk, beaten (optional)

Sesame seeds (optional)

1. Lightly coat a nonstick or silicone muffin pan with nonstick cooking spray.

2. In a large bowl, dissolve the yeast and 1 tablespoon of maple syrup in the water. Stir with a fork until the yeast dissolves and let stand until the yeast foams and is activated, 5 to 10 minutes.

3. Whisk in the eggs, oil, vinegar, remaining maple syrup and milk, and salt until blended. Add the flour blend, baking powder, and xanthan gum. Blend just until a wet dough forms, 3 to 5 minutes.

4. Transfer to the prepared bowl, turn, cover with plastic wrap, and let stand in a warm, draft-free place to rise for 3 hours.

5. Preheat the oven to 375°F.

6. Divide the dough into 12 pieces and shape into 2-inch rounds. Place one round in each muffin cup. Cover with plastic wrap and let rise for 30 minutes.

CONTINUED

7. Brush the tops of the rolls with the water (if using). Sprinkle with sesame seeds (if using). Bake until golden brown, about 20 minutes.

PREP TiP: Do not use too much flour while kneading; otherwise, the dough may be too dense to rise. Add just enough to manage the dough.

STORAGE: Make sure the rolls have cooled completely before storing. Store at room temperature in an airtight container for up to 3 days. If the rolls are hard, microwave for 5 to 10 seconds to soften.

Crunchy Breadsticks

NUT-FREE | SOY-FREE

Greet your guests by offering them a board of charcuterie and antipasti with crispy breadsticks. They are an enjoyable snack to make in advance and have on hand.

PREP TIME: **35 MINUTES, PLUS 1 HOUR AND 10 MINUTES TO RISE**

BAKE TIME: **20 MINUTES**

MAKES
24 BREADSTICKS

2¼ teaspoons instant rise yeast

1 tablespoon light brown sugar or coconut sugar

½ cup lukewarm water

1 large egg

½ cup plain dairy-free yogurt

1 tablespoon extra-virgin olive oil or avocado oil

1 teaspoon dried tarragon

1 teaspoon dried dill

½ teaspoon onion powder

1¾ cups Basic Gluten-Free Flour Blend (page 10) or store-bought equivalent

½ cup tapioca flour

1 teaspoon salt

1. Line a baking sheet with parchment paper or a silicone baking mat.

2. In a large bowl, dissolve the yeast and sugar in the water. Stir with a fork until the yeast dissolves and let stand until the yeast foams and is activated, 5 to 10 minutes. Whisk in the egg, yogurt, oil, tarragon, dill, and onion powder until combined.

3. In a separate large bowl, combine the flour blend, tapioca flour, and salt. Add the yeast mixture and blend to form a dough. With floured hands, knead, adding more flour if needed, until moist but just barely sticky, 6 to 8 minutes. Cover with plastic wrap and set in a warm, draft-free place to rise for 45 minutes.

4. Preheat the oven to 350°F.

5. Divide the dough into 24 balls. Roll each ball into 5-by-1-inch strips. Place on the prepared baking sheet and let rise for 25 minutes.

6. Bake until golden brown, about 20 minutes. Let cool for 5 minutes, then transfer to a wire rack to cool completely.

STORAGE: Store at room temperature in an airtight container for up to 5 days.

Caramelized Onion and Mushroom Pizza with Sweet Nectarines (page 67)

CHAPTER
5

PiZZA, FLATBREADS, AND CRACKERS

There is nothing like a family pizza night or sinking your teeth into a salty, crispy cracker—two of my favorite comfort foods. I still fondly remember a birthday when my mom made me a pizza with my most beloved vegetable toppings. Now, as a mom of two, I enjoy birthday pizza and Friday pizza nights with my family, each of us adding our own toppings to personalize the crusts. And there is no reason not to continue these traditions just because you are gluten-free. You can create any pizza of your liking with my gluten-free pizza dough. And don't stop with pizza. Celebrate summer with s'mores made from homemade graham crackers, or pack your own gluten-free crackers in lunches or for an afternoon wine and cheese picnic.

Gluten-Free Restaurant-Style Pizza Dough

NUT-FREE | SOY-FREE

Use this basic pizza dough recipe for all your pizza needs. It makes two small pizzas. Get the kids involved by having them roll out their own mini pizzas and top the dough with their favorite ingredients.

PREP TIME: 1 HOUR, PLUS 3 HOURS TO RISE

MAKES 2 (12-INCH) CRUSTS

2¼ teaspoons instant rise yeast

2 tablespoons maple syrup, divided

1 cup lukewarm water

4 large eggs

3 tablespoons extra-virgin olive oil or avocado oil

1 teaspoons apple cider vinegar

2 cups Basic Gluten-Free Flour Blend (page 10) or store-bought equivalent

⅓ cup coconut milk powder, egg white powder, or almond meal

½ cup tapioca flour

½ cup potato starch

⅓ cup arrowroot

1 tablespoon xanthan gum or 2 tablespoons psyllium husk

2 teaspoons salt

1. In a small bowl, dissolve the yeast and 1 tablespoon of maple syrup in the water. Stir with a fork until the yeast dissolves, and let stand until the yeast foams and is activated, 5 to 10 minutes.

2. In a separate small bowl, whisk together the eggs, oil, vinegar, and remaining 1 tablespoon of maple syrup.

3. In a large bowl, combine the flour blend, milk powder, tapioca flour, potato starch, arrowroot, xanthan gum, and salt. Make a well in the center of the flour mixture and add the egg mixture and yeast mixture. With a spatula, mix to combine. The mixture will be slightly wet and sticky. Cover with plastic wrap and set in a warm, draft-free place to rise for 3 hours.

4. Lightly coat a large piece of parchment paper with flour.

5. Place the dough on the parchment and knead, adding more flour as needed, until no longer sticky, 8 to 10 minutes. Divide the dough into two disks. Use as directed in the individual recipes.

CONTINUED

Gluten-Free Restaurant-Style Pizza Dough CONTINUED

PREP TiP: To bake the crust, preheat the oven to 500°F. Place a pizza stone or baking sheet in the oven and let it heat up for 30 minutes. Meanwhile, with a lightly floured rolling pin, roll each disk out on parchment paper to a ¼-inch-thick, 12-inch-round circle. Roll the edge over to form the crust. Carefully transfer the parchment paper with the dough to the heated pizza stone. Add your favorite toppings and bake until the crust is slightly browned, 15 to 20 minutes. If you add a lot of toppings, the pizza may need additional baking time. Bake until the liquid from the vegetables evaporates but the crust does not burn.

STORAGE: Store the dough disks in a zip-top bag in the refrigerator for up to 3 days. You can also bake these crusts ahead of time without toppings. Store in the freezer in a zip-top plastic bag for up to 3 months. When ready to use, place on a heated pan or pizza stone and add toppings. Bake at 500°F for 10 to 15 minutes.

Caramelized Onion and Mushroom Pizza with Sweet Nectarines

NUT-FREE | SOY-FREE

Caramelized onions and mushrooms make great toppings for pizza, especially when paired with spicy arugula. Topping it off with thick, sweet balsamic glaze makes for a rich, decadent pie.

PREP TIME: **30 MINUTES**
BAKE TIME: **20 MINUTES**
SERVES 2

4 tablespoons extra-virgin olive oil, divided

½ red onion, thinly sliced

½ cup sliced mushrooms

1 tablespoon light brown sugar or coconut sugar

Kosher salt

½ recipe (1 disk) Gluten-Free Restaurant-Style Pizza Dough (page 65)

1 to 2 cups shredded vegan mozzarella cheese

3 ounces thinly sliced prosciutto

4 cups baby arugula

1 just ripe nectarine, pitted and very thinly sliced

2 tablespoons gluten-free balsamic vinegar glaze

Freshly ground pepper

1. Preheat the oven to 500°F. Lightly flour a piece of parchment paper. Place a pizza stone or baking sheet in the oven to heat for 30 minutes.

2. In a medium saucepan over medium-high heat, heat 1 tablespoon of the oil. Add the onion and mushrooms and cook, stirring frequently, until slightly browned, about 10 minutes. If starting to burn, turn down the heat. Add the sugar and a pinch of salt. Cook, stirring, until the sugar melts. Cook for another 1 minute. Remove from the heat and set aside.

3. With a rolling pin, roll the pizza dough out to a ¼-inch-thick, 12-inch-round disk. If the dough sticks to the pin, flour it slightly. Roll the edge over to form the crust and place on the prepared parchment paper.

4. Carefully transfer the parchment paper with the dough to the heated pizza stone. Bake without toppings for 10 minutes.

5. Remove from the oven. Top with the cheese, caramelized mushrooms and onions, and prosciutto. Return the pizza to the oven; bake until the cheese is golden and bubbly, another 6 to 10 minutes.

CONTINUED

6. Let cool for 5 minutes. Top the pizza with the arugula and nectarine slices. Drizzle with the remaining 3 tablespoons of oil and the balsamic glaze. Season with salt and pepper to taste, slice, and serve.

STORAGE: Store in the refrigerator in an airtight container for up to 3 days.

SUBSTITUTIONS: In cooler months, this pizza is delicious topped with sliced apples or pears instead of the nectarines.

Avocado Crust California Pizza

NUT-FREE | SOY-FREE | VEGAN

This vegan pizza tastes best when eaten immediately. This is one pizza you can feel great about eating—it's loaded with healthy nutrients from the avocado and fresh produce.

PREP TIME: **30 MINUTES, PLUS POTATO COOK TIME**
BAKE TIME: **15 MINUTES**
SERVES 2

1 cup potato starch or tapioca flour, plus more for sprinkling

2 large avocados, peeled and pitted, divided

½ teaspoon freshly squeezed lemon juice

½ teaspoon baking powder

⅛ teaspoon salt

2 to 3 tablespoons water

¾ cup shredded vegan mozzarella cheese

1 Roma tomato, sliced

1 Yukon Gold potato, baked until tender and diced

2 garlic cloves, minced

1 small shallot, thinly sliced

Store-bought vegan pesto (optional)

1 to 2 tablespoons extra-virgin olive oil

Kosher salt

Freshly ground black pepper

VARIATION: For non-vegans, add shredded roasted chicken or crumbled crispy bacon along with the vegetables before baking.

1. Preheat the oven to 500°F. Sprinkle a piece of parchment paper with potato starch. Place a pizza stone or baking sheet in the oven to heat for 30 minutes.

2. In a food processor, combine one of the avocados, the potato starch, lemon juice, baking powder, and salt. Blend until smooth. Slowly add 2 tablespoons of water until it forms a dough. Add 1 more tablespoon of water if needed. The dough should be pliable and soft but not overly sticky.

3. Place the dough on the prepared parchment. Using your hands, press the dough to form a ¼-inch-thick, 12-inch-round disk. Top the dough evenly with the cheese, tomato, potato, garlic, and shallot. Drizzle with the pesto (if using) and oil.

4. Carefully transfer the parchment paper with the dough to the heated pizza stone. Bake until the cheese is golden and bubbly, about 15 minutes.

5. Meanwhile, cube the remaining avocado. Let the pizza cool for 5 minutes, top with the avocado, season with salt and pepper to taste, slice, and serve.

Cauliflower Crust Margarita Pizza

NUT-FREE | SOY-FREE | VEGAN

Cauliflower pizza crusts are quite popular and a great way to enjoy pizza without too many carbs. This one is a favorite of ours, and my kids love theirs topped with pepperoni. The key to a successful crust is to be sure you start with fairly dry cauliflower rice.

PREP TIME: 30 MINUTES
BAKE TIME: 30 MINUTES
SERVES 4

1 head cauliflower, chopped

¼ cup water

1 tablespoon arrowroot

1 tablespoon extra-virgin olive oil or avocado oil

1 tablespoon baking powder

⅔ cup potato starch

1 teaspoon salt, plus more as needed

1 cup shredded vegan mozzarella cheese

1 Roma tomato, sliced

Fresh basil leaves, for garnish

Freshly ground black pepper

1. Preheat the oven to 500°F. Place a pizza stone or baking sheet in the oven and heat for 30 minutes. Flour a piece of parchment paper.

2. Put the cauliflower in a food processor, and process on high until finely chopped and the consistency of rice. Transfer to a medium glass bowl. Microwave on high until tender, 2 to 3 minutes. Let cool until able to handle.

3. Meanwhile, in a small bowl, whisk together the water, arrowroot, oil, and baking powder.

4. Place a nut bag or large dish towel over a large empty bowl. Add the cauliflower rice and squeeze the bag around the cauliflower; water should drain into the bowl. Continue squeezing until the water is removed.

5. In a separate large bowl, combine the cauliflower rice, potato starch, salt, and arrow-root mixture. Stir until a dough forms. If the dough seems too dry to shape, add more water, 1 teaspoon at a time.

6. Place the dough on the prepared parchment. Roll the dough to form a ¼-inch-thick, 12-inch-round disk. Carefully transfer the parchment paper with the dough to the heated pizza stone. Bake for 10 minutes, then carefully flip the crust and bake until lightly golden, about 10 minutes.

7. Top the pizza evenly with the cheese and tomato. Bake until the cheese melts, 5 to 7 minutes. Remove from the oven, garnish with basil, season with salt and pepper to taste, slice, and serve.

STORAGE: Store in the refrigerator in an airtight container for up to 3 days.

SUBSTITUTIONS: Add more of your favorite toppings, such as mushrooms, olive slices, or pepperoni. Or turn it into barbecue chicken pizza by topping with red onion, cooked chicken, gluten-free barbecue sauce, and fresh cilantro.

Sweet Potato–Crusted Pizza with Sun-Dried Tomato Pesto, Portobellos, and Grilled Chicken

SOY-FREE

Pizza does not have to have to be made of only whole grains. Using sweet potatoes for the crust gives this pizza a natural flavor that is packed with extra vitamins and minerals, including potassium. This pizza tastes best when fresh baked.

PREP TIME: **25 MINUTES, PLUS SWEET POTATO COOK TIME**

BAKE TIME: **20 MINUTES**

SERVES 2

For the sun-dried tomato pesto

4 ounces fresh basil leaves (about 2 handfuls)

4 ounces sun-dried tomatoes in olive oil

¼ cup extra-virgin olive oil

¼ cup chopped walnuts

1 tablespoon freshly squeezed lemon juice

1 teaspoon apple cider vinegar

½ teaspoon salt

1 garlic clove, minced

For the sweet potato crust

1 large sweet potato, baked, peeled, and mashed (about 2 cups; see prep tip on page 35)

1 cup potato starch of cornstarch, plus extra for sprinkling

½ teaspoon freshly squeezed lemon juice

1 teaspoon baking powder

⅛ teaspoon salt

1. For the pesto, in a food processor, put the basil, sun-dried tomatoes, oil, walnuts, lemon juice, vinegar, salt, and garlic. Blend on high until smooth. Pour into a small bowl.

2. For the sweet potato crust, preheat the oven to 500°F. Place a pizza stone or baking sheet in the oven to heat for 30 minutes. Sprinkle a piece of parchment paper with potato starch.

3. Wash and dry the food processor bowl. Put the sweet potato, potato starch, lemon juice, baking powder, and salt in the food processor. Pulse until a dough forms.

4. Place the dough on the prepared parchment. Using your hands, press the dough to form a ¼-inch-thick, 12-inch-round disk. Bake for 20 minutes. Lightly spread the pesto over the crust, leaving 1 inch uncovered around the edge.

For the toppings

1 cup diced grilled chicken

½ cup shredded vegan mozzarella cheese

1 portobello mushroom, stemmed and diced

2 tablespoons chopped walnuts

5. For the toppings, sprinkle the chicken, cheese, mushroom, and walnuts over the pesto in the order listed. Bake until slightly browned and most of the liquid from the vegetables evaporates, 10 to 15 minutes. Let cool for 5 minutes, season with salt and pepper to taste, slice, and serve.

SUBSTITUTIONS: This pizza is tasty topped with baby artichokes and olives instead of the mushrooms. You can also use shredded chicken in place of grilled.

Flatbread

NUT-FREE | SOY-FREE | VEGAN

Use this recipe in place of tortillas, as a side bread, or bake it with your favorite pizza toppings. These flatbreads are cooked in a skillet and may start to bubble while cooking, which makes a crisp flatbread.

PREP TIME: **15 MINUTES**
BAKE TIME: **25 MINUTES**

MAKES 4 SMALL FLATBREADS

1¼ cup plain dairy-free yogurt

2 tablespoons plus 4 teaspoons extra-virgin olive oil, divided

1 teaspoon apple cider vinegar

2 cups Basic Gluten-Free Flour Blend (page 10) or store-bought equivalent

¼ cup tapioca flour

1 tablespoon baking powder

1 teaspoon salt

¼ teaspoon baking soda

1. In a large bowl, whisk together the yogurt, 2 tablespoons of oil, and the vinegar. Add the flour blend, tapioca flour, baking powder, salt, and baking soda. With a spatula, stir together until a dough forms. Knead with your hands or the spatula for 3 minutes.

2. Divide the dough into four disks. On a floured work surface, place one of the disks and, using a rolling pin, roll to a ¼-inch thickness. Repeat with the remaining dough disks.

3. In a large nonstick skillet over medium-high heat, heat 1 teaspoon of oil. Add one dough disk to the skillet and cook until slightly browned and crisp, 2 to 3 minutes per side. Transfer to a platter and repeat with the remaining dough, adding 1 teaspoon of oil to the pan for each piece of dough.

STORAGE: Make sure the bread has cooled completely before storing. Store at room temperature in an airtight container for up 3 days. Or store in the refrigerator in an airtight container for up to 1 week.

SUBSTITUTIONS: You can use avocado oil in place of olive oil, as it can withstand higher heat.

Garlic Butter Flatbread Sticks

NUT-FREE | SOY-FREE | VEGAN

These garlic bread sticks are easy to whip up and complement any pasta night or salad when you are craving buttery bread sticks. For a "cheesy" flavor, lightly sprinkle them with nutritional yeast after baking.

PREP TIME: **15 MINUTES**
BAKE TIME: **10 MINUTES**
MAKES 16 STICKS

1 recipe Flatbread (page 74)
4 tablespoons vegan butter, melted
8 garlic cloves, minced
Kosher salt
Freshly ground black pepper

1. Preheat the oven to 400°F. Line a large baking sheet with parchment paper or a silicone baking mat.

2. In a small glass bowl, microwave the butter until melted, about 30 seconds. Stir in the garlic. Place the flatbreads on the prepared baking sheet. With a basting brush, brush them with the garlic butter. Season with salt and pepper to taste. Cut each flatbread into four strips.

3. Bake until crispy, 5 to 10 minutes.

STORAGE: Store in an airtight container in the refrigerator for up to 3 days.

SUBSTITUTIONS: Turn into herbed flatbread sticks by stirring chopped fresh rosemary and oregano in the butter mixture. The butter can also be swapped out for olive oil.

Graham Crackers

NUT-FREE | SOY-FREE

Yes, you can have s'mores, the favorite summertime campfire treats, by sandwiching chocolate and toasted marshmallows between these sweet, crisp crackers. They are also fabulous to snack on, either plain or topped with peanut butter.

PREP TIME: 35 MINUTES
BAKE TIME: 15 MINUTES
MAKES
20 CRACKERS

1½ cups brown rice flour, plus more for sprinkling

½ cup potato starch

⅓ cup packed light brown sugar or coconut sugar

6 tablespoons unsweetened dairy-free milk

5 tablespoons vegan butter

3 tablespoons honey

1 teaspoon baking powder

½ teaspoon salt

1 teaspoon molasses

1 teaspoon granulated sugar (optional)

1. Preheat the oven to 350°F. Lightly flour two pieces of parchment paper.

2. In a food processor, combine the flour, potato starch, sugar, milk, butter, honey, baking powder, salt, and molasses. Pulse until combined. Do not overmix or it will become warm and sticky. If the dough is dry and crumbly, add more milk, 1 teaspoon at a time, until a stiff dough forms.

3. Divide the dough in half and place one piece on one of the prepared pieces of parchment. Pat to form a rectangular shape. Sprinkle the top lightly with more flour and place another piece of parchment paper on top. Roll the dough to an ⅛-inch thickness. Try to keep the dough the same thickness, especially at the edges, to avoid burning. Using a pizza cutter, cut the dough into 2-by-3½-inch rectangles. No need to separate the slices as they will break apart after baking. Repeat this process with the remaining dough.

4. Transfer the dough, on the parchment sheets, to two small baking sheets and place in the freezer for 10 minutes.

5. Remove from the freezer and pierce the tops with several holes using the end of an ice pop stick or fork. This helps make the crackers crisp. Lightly sprinkle the tops with the granulated sugar (if using).

6. Bake until lightly golden, about 15 minutes. Let cool for 10 minutes, then transfer on the parchment to a wire rack to cool completely.

PREP TiP: Freezing the graham crackers before piercing helps the dough hold its shape.

STORAGE: Store at room temperature in an airtight container for up to 1 week.

Gluten-Free Crackers

NUT-FREE | SOY-FREE | VEGAN

Satisfy your salty cravings with these crunchy snacks. They are great to have on hand for wine and cheese parties or as snacks for the kids. They also make delicious dippers for hummus, salsa, or creamy dips.

PREP TIME: 35 MINUTES
BAKE TIME: 15 MINUTES
MAKES
44 CRACKERS

1½ cups brown rice flour, plus more for sprinkling

½ cup potato starch

4 tablespoons vegan butter

6 tablespoons water

1 tablespoon maple syrup

¾ teaspoon salt

½ teaspoon baking powder

Kosher salt

1. Preheat the oven to 400°F. Lightly flour two pieces of parchment paper.

2. In a food processor, combine the flour, potato starch, butter, water, maple syrup, salt, and baking powder. Pulse until combined. Do not overmix or it will become warm and sticky. If the dough is dry and crumbly, add more water, 1 teaspoon at a time, until a stiff dough forms.

3. Divide the dough in half and place one piece on one of the prepared pieces of parchment. Pat to form a rectangular shape. Sprinkle the top lightly with more flour and place another piece of parchment on top. Roll the dough to an ⅛-inch thickness. Try to keep the dough the same thickness, especially at the edges, to avoid burning. Using a pizza cutter, cut the dough into 2-by-3½-inch rectangles. No need to separate the slices as they will break apart after baking. Repeat this process with the second half of the dough.

4. Transfer the dough, on the parchment paper, to two small baking sheets, and place in the freezer for 10 minutes.

5. Remove from the freezer and pierce the top of each rectangle several times with a fork to create holes (like you see on butter crackers). This helps make the crackers crisp. Sprinkle the tops lightly with kosher salt.

6. Bake until slightly browned, about 15 minutes. Let cool for 10 minutes, then transfer on the parchment to a wire rack to cool completely.

STORAGE: Store at room temperature in an airtight container for up to 1 week.

SUBSTITUTIONS: You can use cornstarch in place of potato starch. To make herbed crackers, add 1 teaspoon crushed dried herbs with the ingredients before mixing.

Lemon Bars (page 102)

CHAPTER 6

COOKIES AND BARS

Sweet things, who doesn't love them? I imagine that you, like me when I first started avoiding gluten, thought you'd never be able to have another fudgy, rich chocolate brownie, crispy cookie, or chocolate chip any-thing. Well, think again. This chapter is filled with cookies and bars that wow a crowd. Choose from classic cookies like chocolate chip, peanut butter, or snickerdoodles and rich, gooey bars such as s'mores, brownies, and chocolate chunk blondies. They are all perfect for afternoon snacks, bake sales, or just to fill the cookie jar. There's nothing better than the aroma of fresh baked cookies and bars. My boys love to get off the school bus, open the front door, and smell chocolate chip cookies fresh out of the oven. I hope these sweet baked goodies bring cheerful memories into your home, too.

Giant Chocolate Chip Cookies

NUT-FREE | SOY-FREE

The highlight of any celebration is a moist and chewy chocolate chip cookie that simply melts in your mouth. When eating leftovers, if you'd like that "fresh out of the oven" texture, place a cookie on a plate with a damp paper towel on top, and microwave for 5 to 10 seconds.

PREP TIME: 25 MINUTES, PLUS 1 HOUR TO CHILL
BAKE TIME: 15 MINUTES
MAKES 15 LARGE COOKIES

½ cup vegan butter, melted

½ cup packed light or dark brown sugar or coconut sugar

⅓ cup granulated sugar

1 large egg

1 teaspoon vanilla extract

1⅓ cups Basic Gluten-Free Flour Blend (page 10) or store-bought equivalent

¼ cup potato starch

½ teaspoon baking soda

½ teaspoon salt

10 ounces dairy-free semisweet chocolate chips

1. Preheat the oven to 350°F. Line a baking sheet with parchment paper or a silicone baking mat.

2. In a large bowl, using an electric mixer on low speed, cream the butter, brown sugar, and granulated sugar together. Beat in the egg and vanilla until combined. Add the flour blend, potato starch, baking soda, and salt and beat just until well combined. Stir in the chocolate chips.

3. Cover the bowl with plastic wrap and chill in the refrigerator for 1 hour or overnight.

4. Using a large cookie dough scoop, drop about ¼ cup of dough per cookie and arrange about 2 inches apart on the prepared baking sheet.

5. Bake until slightly browned, about 15 minutes. Let cool for 10 minutes, then transfer to a wire rack to cool completely.

PREP TIP: Chilling the dough is not necessary but keeps the cookies from spreading too thin.

STORAGE: Store at room temperature in an airtight container for up to 3 days.

SUBSTITUTIONS: For smaller cookies, use a 2-inch cookie scoop and bake for 8 to 11 minutes.

Gingerbread Cookies

CONTAINS COCONUT | SOY-FREE | VEGAN

Gingerbread men are another favorite holiday celebration cookie in our house. This dough is wonderful and vegan, so no worries if little mouths want to nibble on the raw dough as you make them.

PREP TIME: **25 MINUTES**
BAKE TIME: **15 MINUTES**
MAKES 15 COOKIES

For the cookies

½ cup maple syrup
⅓ cup molasses
⅓ cup coconut oil, melted
1 teaspoon vanilla extract
1¼ teaspoons baking powder
2½ cups Basic Gluten-Free Flour Blend (page 10) or store-bought equivalent
½ cup tapioca flour
1 teaspoon ground cinnamon
1 teaspoon ground ginger
½ teaspoon salt

For the icing

1 cup confectioners' sugar
3 teaspoons full-fat coconut milk
Sprinkles (optional)

1. For the cookies, preheat the oven to 350°F. Line two baking sheets with parchment paper or silicone baking mats.

2. In a medium bowl, whisk together the maple syrup, molasses, oil, and vanilla. Add the baking powder and whisk well until there are no clumps. Add the flour blend, tapioca flour, cinnamon, ginger, and salt. Stir with a rubber spatula until you can form a ball with the dough. Using your hands, knead the dough until all the flour is worked into it. If the dough is too soft to roll, refrigerate for 30 to 60 minutes.

3. Roll out the dough between two pieces of wax or parchment paper to a ¼-inch thickness. Using cookie cutters, cut the dough into the desired shapes.

4. Carefully place on the prepared baking sheets. Bake for 10 to 12 minutes for soft cookies or 15 minutes for crisp cookies. Let cool for 5 minutes, then transfer to a wire rack to cool completely.

5. For the icing, whisk the sugar and 2 teaspoons of coconut milk together until smooth. Add more of the coconut milk, ½ teaspoon at a time, until thin enough to pipe. Spoon the icing into a small zip-top plastic bag, and snip ⅛ inch from one corner. Pipe the icing onto the cooled cookies and decorate with sprinkles (if using). Let stand for 1 hour to harden.

PREP TIP: If the dough is too dry, add water, 1 teaspoon at a time, until it is workable but not overly sticky.

STORAGE: Store at room temperature in an airtight container for up to 3 days.

Cutout Sugar Cookies

CONTAINS COCONUT | SOY-FREE | VEGAN

These classic holiday cookies are quick to put together and a fun way to get the kids involved in baking! And they are egg-free, so there's no worries about your little ones eating the raw cookie dough!

PREP TIME: **25 MINUTES**
BAKE TIME: **10 MINUTES**
MAKES 24 COOKIES

½ cup maple syrup

¼ cup coconut oil, melted

½ teaspoon vanilla extract

1 cup Basic Gluten-Free Flour Blend (page 10) or store-bought equivalent

⅓ cup tapioca flour

1¼ teaspoons baking powder

¼ teaspoon salt

1. Preheat the oven to 350°F. Line two baking sheets with parchment paper or silicone baking mats.

2. In a large bowl, stir together the maple syrup, coconut oil, and vanilla. Stir in the flour blend, tapioca flour, baking powder, and salt until well blended. If the dough is too sticky, refrigerate for 15 minutes before rolling it out.

3. Roll out the dough between two pieces of wax or parchment paper to a ¼-inch thickness. Using cookie cutters, cut the dough into desired shapes. Arrange about 1 inch apart on the prepared baking sheets.

4. Bake until slightly browned, 8 to 10 minutes. Let cool for 3 minutes, then transfer to a wire rack to cool completely.

PREP TIP: If the dough is too soft to work, roll it on a baking sheet lined with parchment paper and chill in the freezer for 10 minutes before cutting into shapes.

STORAGE: Store at room temperature in an airtight container for up to 1 week.

Peanut Butter Cookies

SOY-FREE

Peanut butter is one of my comfort foods. Add it to cookies in place of flour and I am in heaven. This recipe also works well with almond butter, cashew butter, or sunflower seed butter.

PREP TIME: **25 MINUTES**
BAKE TIME: **15 MINUTES**
MAKES 15 COOKIES

1 cup natural peanut butter

½ cup packed light brown sugar or coconut sugar

½ cup granulated sugar

1 large egg

1 teaspoon vanilla extract

½ teaspoon baking powder

⅛ teaspoon salt

1. Preheat the oven to 325°F. Line a baking sheet with parchment paper or a silicone baking mat.

2. In a large bowl, using an electric mixer on medium speed, beat the peanut butter, brown sugar, granulated sugar, egg, and vanilla together. Add the baking powder and salt and beat until well blended.

3. With a medium cookie scoop, scoop and roll the dough into 1½-inch balls. Arrange about 1 inch apart on the prepared baking sheet. Using the tines of a fork, press the top of each cookie down to form a crisscross pattern.

4. Bake until slightly browned around the edges, 10 to 11 minutes. Let cool for 5 minutes, then transfer to a wire rack to cool completely.

PREP TIP: Do not overmix the batter or it will make a tough cookie.

STORAGE: Store at room temperature in an airtight container for up to 5 days.

Chocolate-Stuffed Chocolate Cookies

NUT-FREE | SOY-FREE

A decadent and chewy chocolate cookie stuffed with dairy-free chocolate chunks is a treat for adults as well as kids. Serve warm so every bite has rich chocolate oozing from the center. To reheat the cookies, bake them in the oven at 350°F for 2 to 3 minutes, or place them in the microwave on a plate with a damp paper towel on top. Cook for 5 to 10 seconds.

PREP TIME: **35 MINUTES, PLUS 1 HOUR TO CHILL**
BAKE TIME: **15 MINUTES**
MAKES 24 COOKIES

1½ cups Basic Gluten-Free Flour Blend (page 10) or store-bought equivalent

½ cup unsweetened cocoa powder

⅓ cup tapioca flour

¼ cup coconut milk powder, egg white powder, or almond meal

1 teaspoon baking soda

1 teaspoon instant coffee

1 teaspoon salt

¾ cup vegan butter, at room temperature

¾ cup packed light brown sugar or coconut sugar

½ cup granulated sugar

2 large eggs

2 teaspoons vanilla extract

1 (10-ounce) bag dairy-free chocolate chunks

1. In a large bowl, combine the flour blend, cocoa, tapioca flour, milk powder, baking soda, instant coffee, and salt. Mix together until blended.

2. In a large bowl, using an electric mixer on low speed, cream the butter, brown sugar, and granulated sugar together. Beat in the eggs and vanilla until combined. Add half the flour mixture at a time and beat just until well combined, scraping the bowl down with a spatula as needed.

3. Cover the bowl and refrigerate until the dough is firm enough to handle, about 1 hour or overnight.

4. Preheat the oven to 350°F. Line two baking sheets with parchment paper or a silicone baking mat.

5. Using a 1-inch cookie scoop, form the dough into 24 balls. Place 12 balls on each of the prepared baking sheets. Split each ball in half, flatten one half with the bottom of a glass on the parchment so it is 2 inches in diameter, and place three chocolate chunks in the middle. Flatten the other half in your hand. Place this half over the chunks, and press the edges together to seal. Refrigerate for 10 minutes.

6. Bake the cookies until the edges start to brown lightly, 11 to 12 minutes. Let cool for 10 minutes, then transfer to a wire rack to cool completely.

STORAGE: Store in an airtight container for up to 3 days. You can also freeze the unbaked cookies on the baking sheet, then transfer them to a zip-top plastic bag in the freezer for up to 2 months. Bake from frozen according to the recipe, adding 5 minutes to the total baking time.

VARIATION: Chop a dairy-free white chocolate bar into chunks and substitute for the chocolate chunks.

Oatmeal-Flax Cookies

CONTAINS COCONUT | SOY-FREE

These crunchy, flavorful cookies are always a hit. I served them at a recent gathering, and many guests asked for the recipe, including a chef who wanted to serve them at a wedding!

PREP TIME: **25 MINUTES**
BAKE TIME: **15 MINUTES**
MAKES **36 COOKIES**

2¾ cups certified gluten-free rolled oats

½ cup plus 2 tablespoons Basic Gluten-Free Flour Blend (page 10) or store-bought equivalent

½ cup flaxseed meal

¼ cup tapioca flour

¾ teaspoon salt

½ teaspoon baking soda

¾ cup coconut oil, melted and lukewarm but not hot

¾ cup packed light brown sugar or coconut sugar

¾ cup granulated sugar

¼ cup unsweetened dairy-free milk

1 large egg

2 teaspoons vanilla extract

1. Preheat the oven to 375°F. Line two baking sheets with parchment paper or silicone baking mats.

2. In a medium bowl, combine the oats, flour blend, flaxseed meal, tapioca flour, salt, and baking soda.

3. In a large bowl, using an electric mixer on low speed, cream the oil, brown sugar, and granulated sugar together until smooth. Beat in the milk, egg, and vanilla until blended. On low speed, beat in the oat mixture just until blended.

4. Drop rounded tablespoonfuls of the dough 2 inches apart on the prepared baking sheets. Bake until golden brown around the edges, 10 to 12 minutes. Let cool for 2 minutes, then transfer to a wire rack to cool completely.

STORAGE: Store at room temperature in an airtight container for up 3 days.

SUBSTITUTIONS: Add some sweetness to these cookies by stirring in ½ cup raisins or dried cranberries with the oat mixture.

Matcha-Coconut Macaroons

CONTAINS COCONUT | SOY-FREE

Chewy coconut flavors these tender cookies and tantalizes the taste buds! For a little extra sweetness, dip the bottoms in melted dairy-free chocolate.

PREP TIME: **25 MINUTES**

BAKE TIME: **15 MINUTES**

MAKES
24 MACAROONS

3 cups unsweetened fine macaroon coconut

4 large egg whites, at room temperature

¾ cup granulated sugar

½ cup coconut milk powder, egg white powder, or almond meal

1 tablespoon matcha green tea powder

1 teaspoon vanilla extract

¼ teaspoon salt

1. Preheat the oven to 350°F. Move the oven rack to the bottom third of the oven. Line a baking sheet with parchment paper or a silicone baking mat.

2. Place the coconut on the prepared baking sheet and bake until toasted, about 2 minutes. Remove from the baking sheet and set it aside.

3. In a large bowl, using an electric mixer on medium speed, beat the egg whites, granulated sugar, milk powder, matcha powder, vanilla, and salt together until combined. Stir in the toasted coconut until well blended.

4. With a medium cookie scoop, scoop and roll the dough into 1½-inch balls. Arrange about 1 inch apart on the prepared baking sheet. Bake until golden brown, 15 minutes. Let cool for 10 minutes, then transfer to a wire rack to cool completely.

PREP TiP: If the dough is sticky, wet your hands slightly when shaping the dough.

STORAGE: Store at room temperature in an airtight container for up to 1 week.

SUBSTiTUTiONS: Not a fan of matcha flavor? Skip the matcha altogether for a coconut-vanilla flavored treat.

Almond Biscotti

SOY-FREE

These Italian cookies are twice baked for an extra-crispy texture and are extra-delicious dipped in chocolate. They are wonderful with coffee in the morning or for an afternoon tea party.

PREP TIME: 25 MINUTES

BAKE TIME: 1 HOUR AND 5 MINUTES

MAKES 22 COOKIES

1 cup Basic Gluten-Free Flour Blend (page 10) or store-bought equivalent

¾ cup almond meal

½ cup potato starch

2 teaspoons baking powder

2 teaspoons xanthan gum

1 teaspoon salt

3 large eggs

⅔ cup packed light brown sugar or coconut sugar

1 teaspoon almond extract

2 cups dairy-free chocolate chunks

1 cup chopped almonds

1. Preheat the oven to 325°F. Line a large baking sheet with parchment paper or a silicone baking mat.

2. In a medium bowl, stir together the flour blend, almond meal, potato starch, baking powder, xanthan gum, and salt.

3. In a separate medium bowl, whisk together the eggs, sugar, and almond extract until well blended. Add to the flour mixture and stir to form a dough. Let the dough stand for 5 minutes.

4. Turn the dough onto the prepared baking sheet and cut in half. Form each half into a 11-by-4-inch log.

5. Bake until slightly browned, 30 to 35 minutes. Let cool for 5 minutes.

6. Cut the logs into 1-inch-thick diagonal slices. Bake until slightly browned, another 25 to 30 minutes. Let cool for 10 minutes, then transfer to a wire rack to cool completely. Set the prepared baking sheet aside.

7. In a shallow glass bowl, microwave the chocolate chunks on high for 30 to 60 seconds, just until starting to melt. Stir to completely melt. Dip one side of the biscotti into the melted chocolate. Sprinkle with the chopped almonds. Return to the prepared baking sheet. Refrigerate until the chocolate is firm.

PREP TiP: Cut the logs with a serrated knife to prevent them from crumbling.

STORAGE: Store at room temperature in an airtight container for up to 5 days, or store in the refrigerator to keep the chocolate from melting.

Snickerdoodles

CONTAINS COCONUT | SOY-FREE | VEGAN

To enjoy them soft and chewy, follow the baking times given. For a crispier cookie, bake for an additional 2 minutes.

PREP TIME: **25 MINUTES**
BAKE TIME: **10 MINUTES**
MAKES **21 COOKIES**

1 tablespoon ground cinnamon

1½ teaspoons granulated sugar

½ cup maple syrup

¼ cup coconut oil, melted

1 tablespoon unsweetened applesauce

½ teaspoon vanilla extract

1½ cups almond meal

½ cup Basic Gluten-Free Flour Blend (page 10) or store-bought equivalent

½ teaspoon baking soda

½ teaspoon cream of tartar

¼ teaspoon salt

1. Preheat the oven to 350°F. Line a large baking sheet with parchment paper or a silicone baking mat.

2. In a small bowl, stir together the cinnamon and sugar.

3. In a medium bowl, whisk together the maple syrup, oil, applesauce, and vanilla. Add the almond meal, flour blend, baking soda, cream of tartar, and salt and stir until well blended. If the dough is too soft to shape, refrigerate until firm, about 30 minutes.

4. With a medium cookie scoop, scoop and roll the dough into 1½-inch balls, then roll in the cinnamon sugar. Arrange about 2 inches apart on the prepared baking sheet. Using the bottom of a glass, press down on the balls slightly.

5. Bake until the cookies begin to crack, about 10 minutes. Let cool for 10 minutes, then transfer to a wire rack to cool completely.

STORAGE: Store at room temperature in an airtight container up to 3 days.

SUBSTITUTIONS: You can omit the cinnamon topping and just roll in plain sugar or combine 1½ teaspoons *each* of unsweetened cocoa powder and ground cinnamon with 2 teaspoons of granulated sugar for a chocolate-cinnamon coating.

Fudgy Chocolate Brownies

CONTAINS COCONUT | SOY-FREE

These dark, rich brownies are sure to please both kids and adults. In fact, they should come with a warning sign, because they are incredibly addictive! Sprinkle the top with chopped walnuts before baking to add a crunch and some heart-healthy benefits.

PREP TIME: **15 MINUTES**
BAKE TIME: **25 MINUTES**

MAKES
24 BROWNIES

1¼ cups dairy-free chocolate chunks, melted
1 cup coconut oil, melted
¼ teaspoon instant coffee
5 large eggs
2 cups packed light brown sugar
1 tablespoon vanilla extract
1 cup sorghum flour
½ cup potato starch
¼ cup tapioca flour
¼ cup unsweetened cocoa powder
½ teaspoon xanthan gum
½ teaspoon salt

1. Preheat the oven to 375°F. Place a rack in the upper third of the oven. Line a 9-by-13-inch baking pan with parchment paper.

2. In a medium glass bowl, combine the chocolate chunks and oil. Microwave for 1 to 2 minutes, stirring every 30 seconds, just until starting to melt. Stir to completely melt, then stir in the instant coffee.

3. In a large bowl, using an electric mixer on high speed, beat the eggs, sugar, and vanilla until light in color and thick, about 10 minutes. On low speed, beat in the melted chocolate mixture. Slowly add the sorghum flour, potato starch, tapioca flour, cocoa, xanthan gum, and salt just until blended, scraping down the sides and bottom of the bowl as needed. Pour the batter into the prepared pan.

4. Bake until the edges are slightly cracked and a toothpick inserted in the center comes out with moist crumbs, about 25 minutes. Let cool for 10 minutes, then use the parchment paper to lift the brownie from the baking pan. Cool on a wire rack for 2 hours before cutting.

PREP TIP: If you like fudgy brownies, don't over-bake them. If you prefer cake-like brownies, add 5 to 10 minutes to the baking time, taking care not to let the sides burn.

STORAGE: Store in an airtight container at room temperature for up to 3 days or in the refrigerator for up to 5 days. To freeze, line aluminum foil with wax paper. Wrap tightly, then transfer to a zip-top plastic bag and freeze for up to 3 months.

SUBSTITUTIONS: You can swap 1¾ cups gluten-free flour mix for the sorghum flour, potato starch, and tapioca flour.

S'mores Brownie Bars

CONTAINS COCONUT | SOY-FREE

Favorite campfire flavors just got a makeover in these delicious chocolatey brownies with a graham cracker base and a topping of toasted marshmallows.

PREP TIME: **20 MINUTES**
BAKE TIME: **30 MINUTES**
MAKES 24 BARS

1 cup plus 2 tablespoons coconut oil, divided

2 cups gluten-free graham cracker crumbs

1 (10-ounce) bag dairy-free chocolate chunks

5 large eggs

2 cups packed light brown sugar

2 teaspoons vanilla extract

1¾ cups Basic Gluten-Free Flour Blend (page 10) or store-bought equivalent

¼ cup unsweetened cocoa powder

½ teaspoon salt

4 cups mini marshmallows

Gluten-free graham cracker, broken into bite-size pieces (optional)

1. Preheat the oven to 375°F. Place a rack in the upper third of the oven. Line a 9-by-13-inch baking pan with parchment paper.

2. In a medium glass bowl, microwave ¼ cup plus 2 tablespoons of oil for 30 seconds, until melted. Stir in the graham cracker crumbs until blended. Press the crumb mixture onto the bottom of the prepared pan to form a crust.

3. In a medium glass bowl, combine the chocolate chunks and remaining ¾ cup of oil. Microwave for 1 to 2 minutes, stirring every 30 seconds, just until starting to melt. Stir to completely melt.

4. In a large bowl, using an electric mixer on high speed, beat the eggs, sugar, and vanilla until light in color and thick, about 10 minutes. On low speed, beat in the melted chocolate mixture. Slowly add the flour blend, cocoa powder, and salt until blended, scraping down the sides and bottom of the bowl as needed. Pour into the prepared pan. Top evenly with the marshmallows; gently press down on them so they partially go into the batter.

5. Bake until the edges are slightly cracked and a toothpick inserted in the center comes out with moist crumbs, about 30 minutes.

6. Let cool for 10 minutes, then use the parchment paper to lift from the baking pan. Cool on a wire rack for 4 hours before cutting.

PREP TiP: Use store-bought gluten-free graham crackers or my recipe on page 76 for the pieces. If you'd like to make your own graham cracker crumbs, put graham crackers in a zip-top plastic bag and crush with a rolling pin.

STORAGE: Store in an airtight container at room temperature for up to 3 days or in the refrigerator for up to 5 days. To freeze, line aluminum foil with wax paper. Wrap tightly, then transfer to a zip-top plastic bag and freeze for up to 3 months.

Chocolate Chunk Blondies

SOY-FREE

Almond and garbanzo bean flours, along with cashews, make these bars a good source of protein and perfect for a playground treat or afternoon pick-me-up. To change them up, you can use dried cranberries or chopped dates in place of the chocolate chunks.

PREP TIME: **15 MINUTES**
BAKE TIME: **25 MINUTES**
MAKES 24 BLONDIES

1 cup garbanzo bean flour

1 cup almond meal

½ cup potato starch

1 teaspoon baking powder

½ teaspoon salt

½ cup vegan butter, at room temperature

2 large eggs

1 large egg white

½ cup packed dark brown sugar or coconut sugar

½ cup granulated sugar

2 teaspoons vanilla extract

¾ cup raw cashew pieces

1 (10-ounce) package dairy-free chocolate chunks

1. Preheat the oven to 350°F. Place a rack in the upper third of oven. Line a 9-by-13-inch baking pan with parchment paper.

2. In a medium bowl, combine the garbanzo bean flour, almond meal, potato starch, baking powder, and salt.

3. In a large bowl, using an electric mixer on medium speed, beat the butter, eggs, egg white, brown sugar, granulated sugar, and vanilla together until blended. On low speed, beat in the flour mixture until blended. Stir in the cashew pieces and chocolate chunks. Pour into the prepared pan.

4. Bake until golden brown and a toothpick inserted in the center comes out with moist crumbs, about 25 minutes. Cool completely in the pan set on a wire rack.

STORAGE: Store in an airtight container at room temperature for up to 3 days or in the refrigerator for up to 5 days. To freeze, line aluminum foil with wax paper. Wrap tightly, then transfer to a zip-top plastic bag and freeze for up to 3 months.

Chocolate Chip Coconut Pecan Pie Bars

CONTAINS COCONUT | SOY-FREE

This delicious alternative to pecan pie has a buttery base and makes a surprising dessert for dinner parties or everyday meals. Adding coconut gives it a lovely texture.

PREP TIME: 15 MINUTES
BAKE TIME: 25 MINUTES
MAKES 16 BARS

2 Sweet Tart Dough disks (page 134)

2 large eggs

¾ cup dark corn syrup

¼ cup packed light or dark brown sugar or coconut sugar

1½ tablespoons coconut oil, melted

1 teaspoon vanilla extract

⅛ teaspoon salt

1½ cups chopped pecans

½ cup unsweetened shredded coconut

½ cup dairy-free mini chocolate chips

1. Preheat the oven to 375°F. Coat a 9-inch square baking pan with nonstick cooking spray.

2. Press both dough disks evenly on the bottom and up the sides of the prepared pan about 1 inch. Bake until slightly browned, about 5 minutes.

3. In a medium bowl, whisk together the eggs, corn syrup, sugar, oil, vanilla, and salt. Stir in the pecans. Pour this mixture into the baked crust. Sprinkle with the coconut and chocolate chips.

4. Bake until a knife inserted in the center comes out clean, about 20 minutes. Transfer the pan to a wire rack to cool completely. Cut into 16 squares, and serve from the pan.

STORAGE: Store in an airtight container at room temperature for up to 3 days or in the refrigerator for up to 5 days. To freeze, line aluminum foil with wax paper. Wrap tightly, then transfer to a zip-top plastic bag and freeze for up to 3 months.

SUBSTITUTIONS: For a more dramatic look, use unsweetened coconut chips in place of the shredded coconut and dairy-free chocolate chunks instead of the mini chips.

Lemon Bars

CONTAINS COCONUT | SOY-FREE

These bars get their rich citrus essence from freshly squeezed lemon juice and a sprinkle of lemon zest. They are best served at room temperature for a softer crust.

PREP TIME: 15 MINUTES
BAKE TIME: 20 MINUTES
MAKES 24 BARS

For the crust

2 cups Basic Gluten-Free Flour Blend (page 10) or store-bought equivalent

½ cup tapioca flour

¼ cup granulated sugar

1 tablespoon flaxseed meal

¼ teaspoon salt

¾ cup vegan butter, melted

For the filling

4 large eggs

1⅓ cups granulated sugar

3 tablespoons Basic Gluten-Free Flour Blend (page 10) or store-bought equivalent

1 teaspoon grated lemon zest

¾ cup freshly squeezed lemon juice

¼ cup canned coconut cream

Confectioners' sugar (optional)

1. For the crust, preheat the oven to 350°F. Lightly coat a 9-by-13-inch baking pan with nonstick cooking spray.

2. In a medium bowl, combine the flour blend, tapioca flour, sugar, flaxseed meal, and salt. Add the butter and mix to form a dough. Using your hands, evenly press the dough into the bottom of the prepared pan. Bake until the edges are slightly browned, about 18 minutes.

3. For the filling, in a medium bowl, whisk together the eggs, granulated sugar, flour blend, lemon zest and juice, and cream until combined. Pour the mixture over the baked crust.

4. Bake until a knife inserted in the center comes out clean, 15 to 20 minutes. Transfer the pan to a wire rack to cool completely. Cut into 24 bars and sprinkle with the confectioners' sugar (if using) just before serving from the pan.

PREP TIP: These bars may split if overcooked. Remove the pan from the oven when the center is slightly firm but before the top has split.

STORAGE: Store in an airtight container in the refrigerator for up to 5 days.

SUBSTITUTIONS: You can swap cashew milk or oat milk for the coconut cream.

Oatmeal Raisin Chocolate Chip Bars

CONTAINS COCONUT | SOY-FREE

I gravitate toward this recipe when I'm craving chewy cookies but also looking for something with heart-healthy fiber. You can make them a bit healthier by substituting dried cranberries for the chocolate chips.

PREP TIME: **15 MINUTES**
BAKE TIME: **30 MINUTES**
MAKES 24 BARS

2 cups certified gluten-free rolled oats

½ cup garbanzo bean flour

½ cup tapioca flour

1 teaspoon xanthan gum

1 teaspoon baking powder

½ teaspoon baking soda

½ teaspoon salt

1 cup vegan butter, at room temperature

2 large eggs, at room temperature

1 cup packed dark brown sugar or coconut sugar

½ cup granulated sugar

2 teaspoons vanilla extract

¾ cup raisins

1 (9-ounce) bag dairy-free chocolate chips

1. Preheat the oven to 350°F. Line a 9-by-13-inch baking pan with parchment paper.

2. In a medium bowl, combine the oats, garbanzo bean flour, tapioca flour, xanthan gum, baking powder, baking soda, and salt.

3. In a large bowl, using an electric mixer on medium speed, beat the butter, eggs, both sugars and vanilla together until creamy. On low speed, beat in the oat mixture just until blended. Stir in the raisins and chocolate chips. Spread in the bottom of the prepared pan and press with spatula to spread evenly.

4. Bake until golden brown and a toothpick inserted in the center comes out with moist crumbs, 25 to 30 minutes. Let cool for 20 minutes, then use the parchment paper to lift from the baking pan and transfer to a wire rack to cool completely before slicing.

STORAGE: Store at room temperature in an airtight container for up to 3 days.

Quick and Easy Energy Bars

SOY-FREE

Energy bars are a healthy way to stay fueled for your day's events, whether it's hiking to the top of the hill, playing with your kids, or simply keeping focused at the office. These make a quick breakfast-on-the-go, as well.

PREP TIME: **15 MINUTES**
BAKE TIME: **25 MINUTES**
MAKES 16 BARS

2 cups certified gluten-free rolled oats

1¼ cups Basic Gluten-Free Flour Blend (page 10) or store-bought equivalent

¾ cup packed light brown sugar or coconut sugar

¼ cup flaxseed meal

½ cup slivered almond

½ cup dried cranberries

¼ cup pumpkin seeds

¾ teaspoon ground cinnamon

¾ teaspoon salt

1 large egg, beaten

½ cup vegan butter or coconut oil, melted and lukewarm but not hot

½ cup honey

2 teaspoons vanilla extract

½ cup dairy-free mini chocolate chips

1. Preheat the oven to 350°F. Line a 9-by-13-inch baking pan with parchment paper.

2. In a large bowl, combine the oats, flour blend, sugar, flaxseed meal, almonds, cranberries, pumpkin seeds, cinnamon, and salt. Make a well in the center and add the egg, butter, honey, and vanilla. Mix well using a large spoon or your hands. Add the chocolate chips and combine.

3. Using your hands, pat the mixture evenly into the prepared pan. Bake until golden brown, about 25 minutes. Let cool for 10 minutes, then use the parchment paper to lift the bars from the baking pan. Transfer to a wire rack to cool completely before slicing.

STORAGE: Store at room temperature in an airtight container for up to 4 days.

SUBSTITUTIONS: You can use chopped walnuts instead of the almonds, raisins in place of the cranberries, and pumpkin pie spice instead of the cinnamon.

Fruit and Oat Crumble Bars

SOY-FREE | VEGAN

Most bake sales don't offer gluten-free treats, but these bars are always a hit—whether the buyer is avoiding gluten or not. For a chocolate treat, use chocolate-hazelnut spread instead of the jam.

PREP TIME: **15 MINUTES**
BAKE TIME: **30 MINUTES**
MAKES 9 BARS

1¼ cups Basic Gluten-Free Flour Blend (page 10) or store-bought equivalent

1¼ cups certified gluten-free quick-cooking oats

½ teaspoon baking soda

¼ teaspoon salt

1 cup packed light brown sugar or coconut sugar

½ cup coconut oil, melted

¼ cup unsweetened dairy-free milk

1 teaspoon vanilla extract

½ cup slivered almonds

8 ounces favorite jam such as strawberry, orange marmalade, peach, blueberry, raspberry, or blackberry

1. Preheat the oven to 350°F. Line a 9-inch square baking pan with parchment paper.

2. In a large bowl, combine the flour blend, oats, baking soda, and salt.

3. In a medium bowl, stir together the sugar, oil, milk, and vanilla. Stir into the flour mixture. Press two-thirds of the mixture in the bottom of the prepared pan. Stir the almonds into the remaining mixture and set aside.

4. Bake until golden brown, about 15 minutes.

5. Remove from oven and spread with the jam. Sprinkle with the reserved almond-oat mixture. Bake until the crumbs are golden brown, 10 to 15 minutes. Let cool for 10 minutes, then use the parchment paper to lift from the baking pan and transfer to a wire rack to cool completely before slicing.

PREP TIP: Quick-cooking oats work best, as they create a fluffy blended crust that holds its shape well.

STORAGE: Store in the refrigerator in an airtight container for up to 5 days.

Red Velvet Cake with Cream Cheese Frosting (page 114)

CHAPTER

7

CAKES AND QUICK BREADS

Even with a gluten intolerance, you can now literally have your cake and eat it too! I have included both a chocolate and a vanilla layer cake, along with favorite flavors like red velvet, lemon, and gingerbread, to name only a few. Thanks to the availability of vegan butters and cream cheese, it is easy to make creamy frostings to top these lovely cakes. You'll also find quick breads that are delicious for a party or hearty enough for breakfast with coffee. For all the gluten-free quick breads, plan to make them a day in advance for easier slicing the next morning.

Pound Cake

SOY-FREE

Moist pound cake filled with buttery flavors is fabulous for a tea party or any celebration, especially topped with a scoop of dairy-free ice cream and a drizzle of dairy-free gluten-free chocolate or caramel sauce.

PREP TIME: **15 MINUTES**
BAKE TIME: **1 HOUR**
SERVES 12

2 cups Gluten-Free Cake and Pastry Flour Blend (page 11) or store-bought equivalent

¼ cup arrowroot

1 tablespoon baking powder

1 teaspoon xanthan gum

¼ teaspoon salt

1 cup honey

1 cup vegan butter, at room temperature

4 large eggs, at room temperature

1 teaspoon apple cider vinegar

1 teaspoon vanilla extract

¼ cup plain dairy-free yogurt

Confectioners' sugar, for dusting

1. Preheat the oven to 350°F. Line a 9-inch loaf pan with parchment paper.

2. In a medium bowl, combine the flour blend, arrowroot, baking powder, xanthan gum, and salt.

3. In a large bowl, using an electric mixer on medium speed, beat the honey and butter together until fluffy, about 3 minutes. On low speed, beat in the eggs, vinegar, and vanilla until combined. Add half the flour mixture and beat to combine. Add the yogurt and beat until blended. Beat in the remaining flour mixture until smooth. Pour into the prepared pan.

4. Bake until a toothpick inserted in the center comes out clean, about 1 hour. Let cool on a wire rack for 20 minutes, then use the parchment paper to lift from the baking pan and transfer to a wire rack to cool completely. Dust with confectioners' sugar before serving.

STORAGE: Store at room temperature in an airtight container for up to 3 days.

VARIATION: Any time a cake crumbles when removing it from a pan too soon, it can easily be turned into a trifle. Layer half the cake in a trifle bowl followed by coconut whipped cream (see page 122) and sliced strawberries. Repeat the layers.

Vanilla Layer Cake with Creamy Vanilla Frosting

SOY-FREE

All celebrations, but especially birthdays, are most festive with a tall layer cake, and being gluten-free and dairy-free shouldn't prevent you from enjoying the fun. Decorate this cake for any occasion with sprinkles, dairy-free chocolate curls, or raspberries.

PREP TIME: 25 MINUTES
BAKE TIME: 25 MINUTES
SERVES 12

For the cake

3¼ cups Gluten-Free Cake and Pastry Flour Blend (page 11) or store-bought equivalent

½ cup almond meal

1 tablespoon baking powder

1 teaspoon baking soda

1 teaspoon xanthan gum

1 teaspoon salt

½ cup vegan butter, at room temperature

2 cups granulated sugar

5 large eggs

1 cup plain dairy-free yogurt

2 teaspoons apple cider vinegar

2 teaspoons vanilla extract

1. For the cake, preheat the oven to 350°F. Lightly coat three 9-inch round cake pans with nonstick cooking spray.

2. In a medium bowl, combine the flour blend, almond meal, baking powder, baking soda, xanthan gum, and salt.

3. In a large bowl, using an electric mixer on medium speed, cream the butter and sugar together until fluffy, about 3 minutes. On low speed, beat in the eggs, yogurt, vinegar, and vanilla until combined, scraping down the sides of the bowl as needed. Beat in the flour mixture until well blended. Divide the batter among the prepared pans.

4. Bake until a toothpick inserted in center comes out clean, 20 to 25 minutes. Let cool for 10 minutes, then carefully remove from the pans and transfer to a wire rack to cool completely.

For the frosting

1 cup vegan butter, at room temperature

¼ to ½ cup unsweetened dairy-free milk

1 tablespoon vanilla extract

5 cups confectioners' sugar

5. For the frosting, in a large bowl, using an electric mixer on high speed, beat the butter, ¼ cup of milk, and the vanilla together until smooth. Beat in the sugar until smooth and spreadable, adding more milk, 1 tablespoon at a time, if too thick. Spread between the layers and over the top and sides of the cake.

STORAGE: Store in an airtight container in the refrigerator for up to 3 days. Also, the cake layers can be made in advance. Seal each cooled layer in a zip-top plastic bag, then refrigerate for up to 2 days or freeze for up to 3 months.

VARIATION: This cake can be turned into cupcakes. Divide the batter between two 12-cup muffin pans lined with paper cups that have been lightly coated with nonstick cooking spray. Bake for 18 to 20 minutes.

Chocolate Layer Cake with Chocolate Frosting

SOY-FREE

There is nothing more decadent than creamy, rich chocolate icing nestled between layers of spongy chocolate
cake. Enjoy this for every celebration when chocolate
is a must!

PREP TIME: **25 MINUTES**
BAKE TIME: **25 MINUTES**
SERVES **12**

For the cake

1½ cups Gluten-Free Cake and
Pastry Flour Blend (page 11) or
store-bought equivalent

1 cup unsweetened cocoa powder

½ cup almond meal

1 tablespoon baking powder

1 teaspoon baking soda

1 teaspoon xanthan gum

1 teaspoon salt

½ cup vegan butter, at room
temperature

1½ cups packed light brown sugar
or coconut sugar

¼ cup maple syrup

5 large eggs

1 cup plain dairy-free yogurt

2 teaspoons apple cider vinegar

2 teaspoons vanilla extract

1. For the cake, preheat the oven to 350°F.
Lightly coat three 9-inch round cake pans with
nonstick cooking spray.

2. In a medium bowl, combine the flour blend,
cocoa, almond meal, baking powder, baking
soda, xanthan gum, and salt.

3. In a large bowl, using an electric mixer
on medium speed, cream the butter, sugar,
and maple syrup together until fluffy, about
3 minutes. On low speed, beat in the eggs,
yogurt, vinegar, and vanilla until combined,
scraping down the sides of the bowl as needed.
Beat in the flour mixture until well blended.
Divide the batter between the prepared pans.

4. Bake until a toothpick inserted in center
comes out clean, 20 to 25 minutes. Let cool
for 10 minutes, then carefully remove from
the pans and transfer to a wire rack to cool
completely.

For the frosting

1 cup vegan butter, at room temperature

¼ to ½ cup unsweetened dairy-free milk

1 tablespoon vanilla extract

5 cups confectioners' sugar

¼ cup unsweetened cocoa powder

5. For the frosting, in a large bowl, using an electric mixer on high speed, beat the butter, ¼ cup of milk, and the vanilla together until smooth. Beat in the sugar and cocoa until smooth and spreadable, adding more milk, 1 tablespoon at a time, if too thick. Spread between the layers and over the top and sides of cake.

STORAGE: Store in an airtight container in the refrigerator for up to 3 days. Also, the cake layers can be made in advance. Seal each cooled layer in a zip-top plastic bag, then refrigerate for up to 2 days or freeze for up to 3 months.

VARIATION: This cake can be turned into cupcakes. Divide the batter between two 12-cup muffin pans lined with paper cups that have been lightly coated with nonstick cooking spray. Bake for 18 to 20 minutes.

Red Velvet Cake with Cream Cheese Frosting

SOY-FREE

This classic Southern cake comes together by adding red food coloring to a light chocolate batter to create a tender, colorful cake that's delicious topped with a sweet cream cheese frosting. Make it into cupcakes for your next bake sale or potluck.

PREP TIME: **25 MINUTES**
BAKE TIME: **25 MINUTES**
SERVES 12

For the cake

2 cups Gluten-Free Cake and Pastry Flour Blend (page 11) or store-bought equivalent

½ cup almond meal

¼ cup unsweetened cocoa powder

1 tablespoon baking powder

1 teaspoon baking soda

1 teaspoon xanthan gum

1 teaspoon salt

½ cup vegan butter, at room temperature

2 cups packed light brown sugar or coconut sugar

5 large eggs

1 cup plain dairy-free yogurt

1 (1-ounce) bottle red food coloring

2 teaspoons apple cider vinegar

2 teaspoons vanilla extract

1. For the cake, preheat the oven to 350°F. Coat three 9-inch round cake pans with nonstick cooking spray.

2. In a medium bowl, combine the flour blend, almond meal, cocoa, baking powder, baking soda, xanthan gum, and salt.

3. In a large bowl, using an electric mixer on medium speed, cream the butter and sugar together until fluffy, about 3 minutes. On low speed, beat in the eggs, yogurt, food coloring, vinegar, and vanilla until combined, scraping down the sides of the bowl as needed. Beat in the flour mixture until well blended. Divide the batter between the prepared pans.

4. Bake until a toothpick inserted in center comes out clean, 20 to 25 minutes. Let cool for 10 minutes, then carefully remove from the pans and transfer to a wire rack to cool completely.

For the frosting

1 cup vegan butter, at room temperature

8 ounces vegan cream cheese

1 tablespoon vanilla extract

5 cups confectioners' sugar

5. For the frosting, in a large bowl, using an electric mixer on high speed, beat the butter, cream cheese, and vanilla together until smooth. Beat in the sugar until smooth and spreadable. Spread between the layers and over the top and sides of cake.

STORAGE: Store in an airtight container in the refrigerator for up to 3 days. Also, the cake layers can be made in advance. Seal each cooled layer in a zip-top plastic bag, then refrigerate for up to 2 days or freeze for up to 3 months.

VARIATION: This cake can be turned into cupcakes. Divide the batter between two 12-cup muffin pans lined with paper cups that have been lightly coated with nonstick cooking spray. Bake for 18 to 20 minutes.

Carrot Cake with Orange Cream Cheese Frosting

SOY-FREE

I think of this cake as man's best friend, because it was my father's favorite and is my husband's most requested dessert. Although it's sweet, it still provides fiber, protein, and healthy fats from the garbanzo bean flour, carrots, pineapple, coconut, and walnuts. My family often enjoys leftovers for breakfast the next morning.

PREP TIME: 25 MINUTES
BAKE TIME: 40 MINUTES
SERVES 16

For the cake

1 cup garbanzo bean flour
½ cup brown rice flour
½ cup almond meal
2 teaspoons ground cinnamon
1 teaspoon baking soda
1 teaspoon xanthan gum
½ teaspoon salt
4 large eggs
1 cup maple syrup
½ cup packed light brown sugar or coconut sugar
1 cup avocado oil
1 teaspoon vanilla extract
3 cups shredded carrots
1 cup chopped walnuts
½ cup drained crushed pineapple
½ cup unsweetened shredded coconut

1. For the cake, preheat the oven to 350°F. Line a 9-by-13-inch baking pan with parchment paper so there is an overhang on two sides.

2. In a medium bowl, combine the garbanzo bean flour, brown rice flour, almond meal, cinnamon, baking soda, xanthan gum, and salt.

3. In a large bowl, whisk together the eggs, maple syrup, sugar, oil, and vanilla. With a spatula, stir in the flour mixture until well blended. Slowly fold in the carrots, walnuts, pineapple, and coconut until fully combined. Pour into the prepared pan.

4. Bake until a toothpick inserted in the center comes out clean, 35 to 40 minutes. Let cool for 10 minutes, then use the parchment paper to lift the cake from the baking pan. Transfer to a wire rack to cool completely.

For the frosting

1 cup vegan butter, at room temperature

8 ounces vegan cream cheese

1 tablespoon vanilla extract

Grated zest of 1 orange (1 teaspoon)

5 cups confectioners' sugar

5. For the frosting, in a large bowl, using an electric mixer on high speed, beat the butter, cream cheese, vanilla, and orange zest together until smooth. Beat in the sugar until smooth and spreadable. Spread over the top of the cake.

PREP TIP: Let the cake cool completely before frosting to prevent the frosting from melting.

STORAGE: Store the unfrosted cake in an airtight container at room temperature for up to 3 days. Store the frosted cake in an airtight container in the refrigerator for up to 3 days.

Lemon Pudding Cake

SOY-FREE

Baking this dessert in a water bath creates a moist cake atop creamy custard—a match made in heaven! You will need a baking pan that is larger than the 9-inch pan to surround the smaller pan with water.

PREP TIME: **15 MINUTES**
BAKE TIME: **40 MINUTES**
SERVES 6

¼ cup garbanzo bean flour

¼ cup almond meal

¼ cup arrowroot

⅛ teaspoon salt

1 cup granulated sugar

1¼ cups canned coconut cream

4 tablespoons vegan butter, melted

⅓ cup freshly squeezed lemon juice

Grated zest of 1 large lemon (1 teaspoon)

1 teaspoon lemon extract

4 large eggs, separated and at room temperature

1 teaspoon cream of tartar

Dairy-free whipped cream, for topping

1. Place a large roasting pan filled halfway with water in the oven. Preheat the oven to 350°F. Lightly coat a 9-inch square baking pan with nonstick cooking spray.

2. In a large bowl, whisk together the garbanzo bean flour, almond meal, arrowroot, and salt. Add the sugar, coconut cream, butter, lemon juice and zest, lemon extract, and egg yolks and whisk until smooth and creamy.

3. In a separate large bowl, using an electric mixer on high speed, beat the egg whites and cream of tartar until soft peaks form. Fold into the lemon mixture until there are no streaks of white. Pour into the prepared pan.

4. Carefully place the baking pan in the roasting pan in the oven; the water should reach halfway up the sides of the baking pan. Bake until the top of the cake is slightly browned and the center of the cake is set, about 40 minutes. Remove from the water bath and place the square pan on a wire rack to cool. Serve warm or at room temperature topped with whipped cream.

STORAGE: Store in the refrigerator in an airtight container for up to 2 days.

Zucchini Bundt Cake

SOY-FREE

This recipe was passed down from my mother to me, and now to you. A family Christmas favorite for more than 20 years, this recipe has been altered to be gluten-free but with the same rich flavors and intense moist texture. Pecans are a delicious alternative.

PREP TIME: **15 MINUTES**
BAKE TIME: **50 TO 55 MINUTES**
SERVES 12

3 cups Gluten-Free Cake and Pastry Flour Blend (page 11) or store-bought equivalent
1 tablespoon baking powder
1½ teaspoons ground cinnamon
1½ teaspoons xanthan gum
1 teaspoon baking soda
1 teaspoon salt
3 large eggs
1 cup packed light brown sugar or coconut sugar
1 cup avocado oil
½ cup maple syrup
1 tablespoon vanilla extract
2 cups grated zucchini, with water squeezed out
½ cup chopped walnuts (optional)

1. Preheat the oven to 350°F. Lightly coat a 9-inch Bundt pan with nonstick cooking spray and dust with flour.

2. In a medium bowl, combine the flour blend, baking powder, cinnamon, xanthan gum, baking soda, and salt.

3. In a large bowl, using an electric mixer on medium speed, beat the eggs until light and creamy. Beat in the sugar, oil, maple syrup, and vanilla until thick and creamy. Stir in the zucchini and flour mixture until well blended. Fold in the walnuts (if using). Pour into the prepared pan.

4. Bake until a toothpick inserted comes out clean, about 50 to 55 minutes. Let cool for 20 minutes on a wire rack, then turn out of the pan onto the rack to cool completely.

PREP TIP: To remove the cake from the pan, run a knife along the edge to loosen before turning the cake out onto the rack.

STORAGE: Store at room temperature in an airtight container for up to 2 days.

VARIATION: Turn this cake into zucchini bread by dividing the batter between two 9-inch loaf pans. Bake for 45 to 55 minutes.

Gingerbread Spiced Bundt Cake

SOY-FREE

Grace your Thanksgiving table with this moist, flavorful cake drizzled with vanilla glaze. Sweetened with molasses and spiked with warming spices like ginger, nutmeg, and cloves, this rich cake is too delicious to save just for the holidays.

PREP TIME: **15 MINUTES, PLUS 1 HOUR TO SET**

BAKE TIME: **60 TO 70 MINUTES**

SERVES 12

For the cake

1½ cups molasses

1 cup hot (not boiling) water

2 cups garbanzo bean flour

1 cup almond meal

1 cup brown rice flour

3 tablespoons psyllium husk

1 tablespoon ground ginger

2 teaspoons baking soda

1 teaspoon ground cinnamon

½ teaspoon ground nutmeg

½ teaspoon ground cloves

½ teaspoon salt

1 cup vegan butter, at room temperature

1 cup packed light brown sugar or coconut sugar

3 large eggs

1 teaspoon vanilla extract

1. For the cake, preheat the oven to 350°F. Lightly coat a 9-inch Bundt pan with nonstick cooking spray and dust with garbanzo bean flour. In a large liquid measuring cup, combine the molasses and water.

2. In a medium bowl, combine the garbanzo bean flour, almond meal, rice flour, psyllium husk, ginger, baking soda, cinnamon, nutmeg, cloves, and salt.

3. In a large bowl, using an electric mixer on medium speed, cream the butter and sugar together. On low speed, beat in the eggs and vanilla until combined. Add half the flour mixture and stir with a spatula until incorporated. Add the molasses-water mixture and remaining flour mixture and stir until smooth and creamy. Pour the batter into the prepared pan.

4. Bake until a toothpick inserted in the center comes out clean, about 60 to 70 minutes. Let cool for 30 minutes on a wire rack, then turn out of the pan onto the rack to cool completely.

For the glaze

1 cup confectioners' sugar

1 to 2 tablespoons unsweetened dairy-free milk

¼ teaspoon vanilla extract

5. For the glaze, 1 hour before serving, in a small bowl, whisk together the sugar, milk, and vanilla until smooth. Drizzle over the cake. Let stand for 1 hour until set.

PREP TIP: Allowing the cake to cool in the pan for 30 minutes helps the cake settle and hold its shape. To remove it from the pan, run a knife around the edge to loosen before turning the cake out onto the rack.

STORAGE: Store at room temperature in an airtight container for up to 3 days.

SUBSTITUTIONS: You can swap 3½ cups gluten-free flour blend for the flours, but it will yield a slightly drier cake.

Angel Food Cake with Coconut Whipped Cream and Strawberries

SOY-FREE

This light and fluffy cake is a hit at Memorial Day and Fourth of July parties, topped with strawberries and blueberries for a festive treat. When beating the egg white mixture, to test for stiff, glossy peaks, rub a little bit of the mixture between your fingers—you'll know it's ready when you don't feel any sugar granules.

PREP TIME: **30 MINUTES**
BAKE TIME: **45 MINUTES**
SERVES 12

For the cake

1½ cups granulated sugar, divided
¾ cup sweet white rice flour
½ cup potato starch
¼ cup tapioca flour
2 teaspoons xanthan gum
12 large egg whites, at room temperature
1½ teaspoons vanilla extract
¼ teaspoon almond extract
½ teaspoon salt
1 teaspoon cream of tartar

For the coconut whipped cream and strawberries

1 (13.5-ounce) can coconut cream or full-fat coconut milk, chilled for 24 hours
½ cup confectioners' sugar
½ teaspoon vanilla extract
4 cups sliced strawberries

1. For the cake, preheat the oven to 325°F. Do not grease the angel food cake pan.

2. Sift ¾ cup of the sugar, the rice flour, potato starch, tapioca flour, and xanthan gum into a medium bowl.

3. In a large bowl, using an electric mixer on medium-high speed, beat the egg whites, vanilla, almond extract, and salt together until foamy. Add the cream of tartar and beat until soft peaks form. Continue beating while gradually add the remaining sugar, ¼ cup at a time, until incorporated. Continue to beat until stiff, glossy peaks form.

4. Sift one-third of the flour mixture over the egg white mixture. Carefully fold it in with a spatula until incorporated. Repeat this process twice with the remaining flour mixture. Pour the batter into the pan. Run a knife through the center of the batter to release any air bubbles. Smooth the top with a spatula for even baking.

5. Bake until the top is lightly golden and cracked and a toothpick inserted in the center comes out with just a few crumbs, 35 to 45 minutes. Turn the pan upside down on a wire rack, the neck of a tall wine bottle, or the feet of the pan (if it has them). Let cool completely for 2 hours. Run a knife carefully around the inside edge of the pan to loosen the cake, then turn it out onto a wire rack.

6. For the coconut whipped cream, turn the can of coconut cream upside down to open. Drain and discard the water. Scoop the cream into a large bowl. Using an electric mixer on high speed, beat until it has the consistency of whipped cream, about 5 minutes. Add the sugar and vanilla and beat for 1 minute, until blended.

7. Slice and serve the angel food cake with a dollop of whipped cream topped with the strawberries.

PREP TIPS:

- Make sure not to grease the pan, because the fat will deflate the egg whites.

- If you use a stand mixer, use the whisk attachment to beat the eggs.

- When folding the flour into the eggs, be sure not to stir too vigorously, or you will deflate the egg whites.

Lemon-Raspberry Quick Bread

NUT-FREE | SOY-FREE

Although they come together quickly, gluten-free quick breads are best baked the day before eating. Allowing the loaf to stand overnight keeps it from crumbling when slicing.

PREP TIME: 15 MINUTES, PLUS OVERNIGHT TO SET

BAKE TIME: 1 HOUR

SERVES 12

¾ cup sweet white rice flour

½ cup sorghum flour

¼ cup potato starch

1 tablespoon baking powder

1½ teaspoons xanthan gum

Grated zest of 2 large lemons (2 teaspoons)

½ teaspoon baking soda

¼ teaspoon salt

1 cup granulated sugar

2 large eggs

½ cup vegan butter, melted

½ cup vanilla dairy-free yogurt

2 tablespoons freshly squeezed lemon juice

½ teaspoon lemon extract (optional)

1½ cups raspberries

1. Preheat the oven to 350°F. Line a 9-inch loaf pan with parchment paper so there is an overhang on two sides.

2. In a medium bowl, combine the rice flour, sorghum flour, potato starch, baking powder, xanthan gum, lemon zest, baking soda, and salt.

3. In a large bowl, whisk together the sugar, eggs, butter, yogurt, lemon juice, and lemon extract (if using). Stir in the flour mixture just until moistened. Carefully fold in the raspberries. Spoon the batter into the prepared pan.

4. Bake until a toothpick inserted in the center comes out clean, about 1 hour, covering with aluminum foil after 45 minutes of baking. Let cool on a wire rack for 20 minutes, then use the parchment paper to lift it from the baking pan and transfer to the rack to cool completely. Wrap and store overnight for best slicing.

PREP TIP: Carefully fold in the raspberries, or they will break, turning the bread pink.

STORAGE: Store the loaf whole, tightly wrapped in a piece of aluminum foil lined with wax paper. Once sliced, store at room temperature in an airtight container for up to 3 days. Or freeze the foil-wrapped loaf or slices in a zip-top plastic bag for up to 3 months.

Pumpkin Quick Bread

NUT-FREE | SOY-FREE

My friend's family loves this recipe and enjoys making it into muffins—it's easy to see why. Whether a loaf or muffins, the results are extremely moist and light with warm, cozy spices.

PREP TIME: **15 MINUTES, PLUS OVERNIGHT TO SET**

BAKE TIME: **55 MINUTES**

SERVES 12

1⅓ cups Basic Gluten-Free Flour Blend (page 10) or store-bought equivalent

2 teaspoons baking powder

1 teaspoon ground nutmeg

1 teaspoon ground cinnamon

1 teaspoon salt

1 (15-ounce) can pumpkin purée (not pumpkin pie filling)

1 cup packed light brown sugar or coconut sugar

4 large eggs

1. Preheat the oven to 350°F. Line a 9-inch loaf pan with parchment paper so there is an over hang on two sides.

2. In a medium bowl, combine the flour blend, baking powder, nutmeg, cinnamon, and salt.

3. In a large bowl, using an electric mixer on medium speed, beat the pumpkin purée and sugar together until blended. Beat in the eggs until well combined. On low speed, add the flour mixture in three additions, beating just until combined. Spoon into the prepared pan.

4. Bake until a toothpick inserted in the center comes out clean, 50 to 55 minutes. Let cool on a wire rack for 20 minutes, then remove the bread by lifting the parchment paper. Transfer to the rack and let cool completely. Wrap and store overnight for best slicing.

PREP TIP: Check the bread for burning after 40 minutes, and, if needed, cover lightly with foil to finish baking.

STORAGE: Store the loaf whole, tightly wrapped in a piece of aluminum foil lined with wax paper. Once sliced, store at room temperature in an airtight container for up to 3 days. Or freeze the foil-wrapped loaf or slices in a zip-top plastic bag for up to 3 months.

Banana-Nut Bread

SOY-FREE

A loaf of this nut-studded bread is a winning gift for friends and family welcoming a new baby or moving into a new home. Be sure to bake it the day before delivering, so the bread can set and will slice up nicely.

PREP TIME: **15 MINUTES, PLUS OVERNIGHT TO SET**
BAKE TIME: **55 MINUTES**
SERVES 12

3 ripe bananas

2 cups Basic Gluten-Free Flour Blend (page 10) or store-bought equivalent

1 tablespoon baking powder

1 teaspoon ground cinnamon

½ teaspoon salt

⅛ teaspoon ground ginger

2 large eggs

⅔ cup maple syrup

½ cup plain dairy-free yogurt

1 tablespoon vanilla extract

¾ cup chopped walnuts, divided

1. Preheat the oven to 350°F. Line a 9-inch loaf pan with parchment paper so there is an overhang on two sides.

2. In a small bowl with a fork, mash the bananas until creamy and blended.

3. In a medium bowl, combine the flour blend, baking powder, cinnamon, salt, and ginger.

4. In a large bowl, using an electric mixer on medium speed, beat the eggs, maple syrup, yogurt, and vanilla together until well blended. Beat in the mashed bananas until combined. On low speed, beat in the flour mixture just until combined. Fold in ½ cup of walnuts. Spoon the batter into the prepared pan. Sprinkle the remaining ¼ cup of walnuts over the top.

5. Bake until a toothpick inserted in the center comes out clean, 50 to 55 minutes. Let cool on a wire rack for 20 minutes, then remove the bread by lifting the parchment paper. Transfer to the rack and let cool completely.

STORAGE: Store the loaf whole, tightly wrapped in a piece of aluminum foil lined with wax paper. Once sliced, store at room temperature in an airtight container for up to 3 days. Or freeze the foil-wrapped loaf or slices in a zip-top plastic bag up to 3 months.

Cherry, Orange, and Pistachio Quick Bread with Orange Glaze

SOY-FREE

This is a moist and delicious bread with hints of orange and pistachio flavor and the tang of cherry bits.

PREP TIME: **15 MINUTES, PLUS OVERNIGHT TO SET**
BAKE TIME: **55 MINUTES**
SERVES 12

For the cake

2 cups Basic Gluten-Free Flour Blend (page 10) or store-bought equivalent

1 tablespoon baking powder

Grated zest of 2 oranges (2 teaspoons)

½ teaspoon salt

2 large eggs

½ cup maple syrup

¾ cup freshly squeezed orange juice

¼ cup avocado oil

1 cup coarsely chopped pitted fresh cherries

¾ cup chopped pistachios

For the glaze

1 cup confectioners' sugar

1 to 2 tablespoons freshly squeezed orange juice

Grated zest of 1 orange (1 teaspoon)

1. For the cake, preheat the oven to 350°F. Line a 9-inch loaf pan with parchment paper so there is an overhang on two sides.

2. In a medium bowl, combine the flour blend, baking powder, orange zest, and salt.

3. In a large bowl, whisk the eggs, maple syrup, orange juice, and oil. Stir in the flour mixture just until combined. Carefully fold in the cherries and pistachios. Spoon into the prepared pan.

4. Bake until a toothpick inserted in the center comes out clean, 50 to 55 minutes. Let cool on a wire rack for 20 minutes, then remove the bread by lifting the parchment paper. Transfer to the rack to cool completely. Wrap and store overnight for best slicing.

5. For the glaze, 1 hour before serving, in a small bowl, whisk together the sugar, orange juice, and zest until smooth. Drizzle over the bread. Let stand for 1 hour until set.

STORAGE: Store the loaf whole, tightly wrapped in a piece of aluminum foil lined with wax paper. Once sliced, store at room temperature in an airtight container for up to 3 days. Or freeze the foil-wrapped loaf or slices in a zip-top plastic bag for up to 3 months.

SUBSTITUTIONS: Use fresh cranberries instead of the cherries.

Lemon-Poppy Seed Bread

NUT-FREE | SOY-FREE

Quick breads are one of my favorite things to make. They are so simple and delicious served with butter or jam for breakfast or a snack. My friends seem to gravitate toward this one, which has the classic flavor combination of lemon and poppy seed.

PREP TIME:
15 MINUTES, PLUS OVERNIGHT TO SET
BAKE TIME: **55 MINUTES**
SERVES 12

1¾ cups Basic Gluten-Free Flour Blend (page 10) or store-bought equivalent

¼ cup potato starch

1 tablespoon baking powder

Grated zest of 2 large lemons (2 teaspoons)

1½ teaspoons xanthan gum

½ teaspoon salt

3 large eggs

½ cup vegan butter, at room temperature

1 cup honey

⅓ cup plain dairy-free yogurt

¼ cup freshly squeezed lemon juice

½ teaspoon vanilla extract

1 teaspoon lemon extract

1 tablespoon poppy seeds

1. Preheat the oven to 350°F. Lightly coat a 9-inch loaf pan with nonstick cooking spray.

2. In a medium bowl, combine the flour blend, potato starch, baking powder, lemon zest, xanthan gum, and salt.

3. In a large bowl, whisk together the eggs, butter, honey, yogurt, lemon juice, vanilla, and lemon extract. Stir in the flour mixture just until combined. Fold in the poppy seeds just until blended. Spoon the batter into the prepared pan.

4. Bake until a toothpick inserted in the center comes out clean, 50 to 55 minutes. Let cool on a wire rack for 20 minutes, then remove the bread from the pan and place it on the rack to cool completely. Wrap and store overnight for best slicing.

PREP TIP: Be careful not to overmix, or the poppy seeds will brown the batter.

STORAGE: Store the loaf whole, tightly wrapped in a piece of aluminum foil lined with wax paper. Once sliced, store at room temperature in an airtight container for up to 3 days. Or freeze the foil-wrapped loaf or slices in a zip-top plastic bag up to 3 months.

Skillet Corn Bread

NUT-FREE | SOY-FREE

This corn bread is a fabulous addition to any meal. This version is mildly sweet, tender, and moist with a slightly crispy crust.

PREP TIME: **15 MINUTES**
BAKE TIME: **30 MINUTES**
SERVES 8

2 cups white or yellow cornmeal

½ cup Basic Gluten-Free Flour Blend (page 10) or store-bought equivalent

½ cup tapioca flour

3 tablespoons psyllium husk

1 tablespoon baking powder

1½ teaspoons xanthan gum

½ teaspoon salt

¼ teaspoon baking soda

2 large eggs

½ cup vegan butter, at room temperature

½ cup honey

2 tablespoons molasses

1½ to 2 cups unsweetened dairy-free milk

1. Preheat the oven to 375°F. Lightly coat a 9-inch cast iron skillet with nonstick cooking spray.

2. In a medium bowl, combine the cornmeal, flour blend, tapioca flour, psyllium husk, baking powder, xanthan gum, salt, and baking soda.

3. In large bowl, using an electric mixer on medium speed, beat the eggs, butter, honey, molasses, and 1½ cups of milk together until well mixed. Stir in the flour mixture just until combined. The batter should be smooth with a cake batter consistency. Add additional milk, 1 tablespoon at a time, if necessary. Pour the batter into the prepared skillet.

4. Bake until the top is golden brown and a toothpick inserted in the center comes out with just a few crumbs, about 30 minutes. Let cool for 5 minutes before cutting into wedges and serving directly from the pan.

STORAGE: Store at room temperature in an airtight container for up to 3 days.

SUBSTITUTIONS: This cornbread can be turned into muffins. Spoon the batter into a 12-cup muffin pan lined with paper cups that have been lightly coated with nonstick cooking spray. Bake for 18 to 22 minutes.

Double Chocolate Tart with Raspberries and Coconut Whipped Cream (page 142)

CHAPTER 8

SWEET AND SAVORY PIES AND FRUIT DESSERTS

These simple pies, tarts, and quiches are luscious, elegant, and a beautiful addition to any table. I hope you celebrate summer with a blackberry galette and key lime pie, fill the holiday season with pumpkin pie and fruit crumble, and end a long weekend with the luxury of an easy savory quiche. Pies take time and more effort than other baked goods, but they are worth the work with every flaky, satisfying bite. In addition, I've included recipes for cobblers, crisps, and rice pudding—some of the most comforting of desserts.

Basic Gluten-Free Pie Dough

SOY-FREE

Use this crust for all your pie needs, both sweet and savory. It's a good basic crust that can also be used for quiches and bars.

PREP TIME: **10 MINUTES, PLUS 30 MINUTES TO CHILL**

MAKES 2 (9-INCH) PIE CRUSTS OR 1 (9-INCH) DOUBLE CRUST

1 large egg

½ teaspoon apple cider vinegar

¼ cup ice water

2 cups Gluten-Free Cake and Pastry Flour Blend (page 11) or store-bought equivalent

1 teaspoon granulated sugar

1 teaspoon xanthan gum

¾ teaspoon salt

¾ cup vegan butter, cut into 1-tablespoon slices and frozen for 10 minutes

1. In a small bowl, whisk the egg, vinegar, and water together.

2. In a large bowl, sift the flour blend, sugar, xanthan gum, and salt together. Using a pastry blender or two knives, cut in the butter until crumbly with pea-size chunks. With a fork, stir in the egg mixture until the dough is moist and can be formed into a ball.

3. Divide the dough into two disks, wrap each in plastic wrap, and refrigerate for 30 minutes or until ready to use. Use as directed in the individual recipe.

PREP TIP: Freezing the butter for 10 minutes before using will result in a flakier piecrust.

STORAGE: Store the wrapped disks in the refrigerator for up to 3 days or in a zip-top plastic bag in the freezer up to 1 month. Thaw in the refrigerator overnight before using.

Sweet Tart Dough

SOY-FREE | VEGAN

This dough is perfect to use in sweet tart recipes and is similar to a basic piecrust, only with more sugar. It also contains no egg, making it a great choice for vegan pies.

PREP TIME: 10 MINUTES, PLUS 30 MINUTES TO CHILL

MAKES 3 (9-INCH) TART SHELLS

3 cups Gluten-Free Cake and Pastry Flour Blend (page 11) or store-bought equivalent

¼ cup tapioca flour

⅓ cup maple syrup

1½ teaspoons xanthan gum

½ teaspoon apple cider vinegar

1½ cups vegan butter, cubed and frozen for 10 minutes

¼ cup ice water

1. In a food processor, pulse the flour blend, tapioca flour, maple syrup, xanthan gum, vinegar, and butter together until it forms coarse crumbs. Add the ice water and pulse again until fine crumbs form. Be careful not to overmix.

2. Transfer the dough to a floured work surface and knead until it forms a ball. Divide into three portions. Form each portion into a disk, wrap in plastic, and refrigerate for 30 minutes before using. Use as directed in the individual recipe.

PREP TIP: Take care not to overmix. You want the dough to resemble small crumbs before being formed into disks.

STORAGE: Store the wrapped disks in the refrigerator for up to 3 days or in a zip-top plastic bag in the freezer up to 1 month. Thaw in the refrigerator overnight before using.

Double-Crusted Berry Pie

SOY-FREE

You can use any mix of berries here, just be sure to use 3 pounds. Adding lemon juice helps bring out the berries' distinct flavor.

PREP TIME: 15 MINUTES, PLUS 4 HOURS TO CHILL

BAKE TIME: 55 MINUTES

SERVES 8

1 pound blueberries

1 pound raspberries

1 pound strawberries, hulled and diced

½ cup packed light brown sugar or coconut sugar

2 tablespoons cornstarch

1 tablespoon freshly squeezed lemon juice

½ teaspoon salt

2 disks Basic Gluten-Free Pie Dough (page 100)

1½ tablespoons coconut oil, melted

1 large egg yolk

1 tablespoon unsweetened dairy-free milk

STORAGE: Store covered at room temperature for up to 3 days.

VARIATION: Add 1 teaspoon of ground cardamom to the berries.

1. In a large bowl, stir together the blueberries, raspberries, strawberries, sugar, cornstarch, lemon juice, and salt.

2. On a lightly floured work surface, roll out one of the dough disks to a 12-inch circle. Transfer to a 9-inch pie pan and press into the bottom and sides. Fill with the berry mixture. Add dots of the oil on top of the berries.

3. On a lightly floured work surface, roll out the remaining disk to form a 12-inch circle. Place over the filling, trim any excess, and seal and crimp the edges. Cut 3-inch slits on the top of the pie to allow the steam to escape. Refrigerate for 15 minutes.

4. Preheat the oven to 400°F. Place a baking sheet on a bottom rack to catch any bubbling juices.

5. In a small bowl, whisk the egg yolk and milk together, and brush over the top of the pie. Place the pie on the center rack of the oven and bake for 20 minutes. Tent it with aluminum foil, allowing air to still flow through, and bake until slightly browned and bubbling in the center, another 35 to 40 minutes. Transfer to a wire rack to cool completely before slicing.

Marbled Chocolate and Peanut Butter Pie

SOY-FREE

Chocolate and peanut butter is a combination that's hard to resist. This pie is suitable for all occasions, from a simple dinner to a birthday party celebration. For special events, you can garnish it with coconut whipped cream (see page 122) and dairy-free chocolate curls.

PREP TIME: **15 MINUTES, PLUS 4 HOURS TO CHILL**
BAKE TIME: **55 MINUTES**
SERVES 8

1 disk Basic Gluten-Free Pie Dough (page 133)
2 cups vegan cream cheese, at room temperature
3 large eggs
1 cup natural peanut butter
¼ cup light brown sugar or coconut sugar
3 tablespoons arrowroot
1 tablespoon coconut oil, melted
2 teaspoons vanilla extract
¼ teaspoon salt
½ cup dairy-free chocolate chips

1. Preheat the oven to 350°F.

2. On a lightly floured work surface, roll out the dough to a 12-inch circle. Transfer to a 9-inch pie pan and press into the bottom and sides. Crimp the edges, then prick the bottom a few times with a fork. Bake until golden, about 10 minutes. Transfer to a wire rack to cool.

3. In a large bowl, using an electric mixer on medium speed, beat the cream cheese until smooth and fluffy. Beat in the eggs, peanut butter, sugar, arrowroot, oil, vanilla, and salt until well blended.

4. In a medium glass bowl, heat the chocolate chips in the microwave for 30 to 60 seconds, just until they start to melt. Stir the chocolate until it is completely melted, then stir in 1 cup of the peanut butter mixture. Pour the remaining peanut butter mixture into the cooled crust. Drop the chocolate mixture by tablespoons over the peanut butter layer, then drag the blade of a knife through the chocolate to swirl it and create a marbled effect.

5. Bake until the filling is firm around the edges, about 45 minutes. It will be slightly soft in the middle and will continue to set as it cools. Transfer to a wire rack to cool completely. Refrigerate for at least 4 hours before serving.

PREP TIP: When marbling the chocolate, be careful not to overwork it to keep the mixtures from blending together—you want to see the marbling.

STORAGE: Store covered in refrigerator for up to 3 days.

SUBSTITUTIONS: You can swap out the peanut butter for almond butter.

Key Lime Pie

SOY-FREE

The tart flavor of little key limes complements the sweetness of maple syrup and creaminess of coconut milk. It is like spending a blissful moment in the tropics.

PREP TIME: **20 MINUTES, PLUS 2 HOURS TO CHILL**
BAKE TIME: **50 MINUTES**
SERVES 6 TO 8

1 disk Basic Gluten-Free Pie Dough (page 133)
2 teaspoons unflavored gelatin
2 tablespoons warm water
½ cup full-fat coconut milk
6 large egg yolks
½ cup plus ⅓ cup granulated sugar, divided
½ cup freshly squeezed key lime juice
Grated zest of 3 key limes (2 teaspoons)
3 large egg whites
½ teaspoon vanilla extract
½ teaspoon cream of tartar

1. Preheat the oven to 350°F.

2. On a lightly floured work surface, roll out the dough to a 12-inch circle. Transfer to a 9-inch pie pan and press into the bottom and sides. Crimp the edges, then prick the bottom a few times with a fork. Bake until golden, about 10 minutes. Transfer to a wire rack to cool.

3. Meanwhile, in a small bowl, mix together the gelatin and water until thickened.

4. In a large bowl, using an electric mixer on low speed, beat the coconut milk, egg yolks, ½ cup of sugar, the gelatin mixture, lime juice, and lime zest together until combined. Pour into the cooled piecrust.

5. Bake until a knife inserted in the center comes out clean, 20 to 25 minutes. Transfer to a wire rack to cool.

6. For the meringue, in a large bowl with an electric mixer on high speed, beat the egg whites, vanilla, and cream of tartar together until foamy. Slowly add the remaining ⅓ cup sugar, about 2 tablespoons at a time, beating until soft peaks form. Spread the meringue over the pie to cover it evenly. Be sure to cover to the crust edges; this will keep the filling from seeping out.

7. Bake until the meringue peaks are lightly golden brown, 12 to 15 minutes. Transfer the pie to a wire rack to cool completely. Refrigerate for at least 2 hours before serving.

PREP TIP: Make sure not to overmix the meringue; whip only until soft peaks form.

STORAGE: Store covered in the refrigerator for up to 3 days.

VARIATION: Use lemon juice and zest in place of the key lime for lemon meringue pie.

Pumpkin Pie

SOY-FREE

This reminds me of the years my mother-in-law baked all the pumpkin pies. Her countertop would be filled with six to eight pies, and the house was filled with the aromas of the season. It is wonderful topped with coconut whipped cream (see page 122).

PREP TIME: **20 MINUTES**
BAKE TIME: **1 HOUR**
SERVES 8

1 disk Basic Gluten-Free Pie Dough (page 133)
½ cup packed light brown sugar or coconut sugar
1 (15-ounce) can pumpkin purée (not pumpkin pie filling)
¾ cup canned full-fat coconut milk
2 large eggs
1 teaspoon vanilla extract
1 teaspoon ground cinnamon
½ teaspoon ground ginger
¼ teaspoon ground cloves
½ teaspoon salt
1 teaspoon vanilla extract

1. Preheat the oven to 350°F.

2. On a lightly floured work surface, roll out the dough to a 12-inch circle. Transfer to a 9-inch pie pan and press into the bottom and sides. Crimp the edges, then prick the bottom a few times with a fork. Bake until golden, about 10 minutes. Transfer to a wire rack to cool.

3. Increase the oven temperature to 375°F.

4. In a large bowl, using an electric mixer on medium speed, beat the sugar, pumpkin purée, coconut milk, eggs, vanilla, cinnamon, ginger, cloves, and salt together until well blended. Pour into the cooled piecrust.

5. Bake until a knife inserted in the center comes out clean, about 50 minutes. Transfer to a wire rack to cool completely.

PREP TiP: Make sure to prick the bottom of the pie crust with a fork or use pie weights over parchment paper. This prevents the crust from puffing up.

STORAGE: Store covered in the refrigerator for up to 5 days.

VARIATION: Add 1½ teaspoons grated orange zest to the pumpkin mixture, and garnish with coconut whipped cream (see page 122) and orange curls.

Blackberry Galette

SOY-FREE

This is a rustic free-form pie that falls naturally in place when the edges of the pastry are folded over. I like to dust the crust with a sprinkle of sugar to enhance blackberry's naturally sweet flavor. This tart is delectable served warm with a scoop of dairy-free vanilla ice cream or coconut whipped cream (see page 122).

PREP TIME: 15 MINUTES
BAKE TIME: 50 MINUTES
SERVES 6 TO 8

1 disk Basic Gluten-Free Pie Dough (page 133)

4 cups blackberries

⅓ cup granulated sugar, plus more for sprinkling

1 tablespoon cornstarch

1 tablespoon freshly squeezed lemon juice

½ teaspoon salt

1 large egg yolk

1 tablespoon unsweetened dairy-free milk

1. Preheat the oven to 375°F.

2. On a lightly floured piece of parchment paper, roll out the dough to a 13-inch circle. Transfer the dough on the parchment to a rimmed baking sheet. Refrigerate while preparing the filling.

3. In a large bowl, carefully toss together the blackberries, sugar, cornstarch, lemon juice, and salt. Remove the crust from the refrigerator. Arrange the fruit in the center, leaving a 1½-inch border all around. Fold the border over the filling, allowing the dough to fall naturally.

4. In a small bowl, whisk together the egg yolk and milk. Brush over the edges of the galette, and sprinkle lightly with sugar.

5. Bake until the crust is golden brown and the filling is bubbling, about 50 minutes. Transfer to a wire rack to cool for 15 minutes before slicing.

PREP TIP: Make sure to use a baking sheet with a rim. This prevents any juices from dripping onto the oven floor and burning.

STORAGE: Store covered at room temperature for up to 3 days.

Double Chocolate Tart with Raspberries and Coconut Whipped Cream

SOY-FREE

A rich chocolate indulgence, this tart is perfect for special events or holidays. Silky custards, like the chocolate one in this tart, are thickened with eggs. To prevent them from curdling after adding them to the hot chocolate mixture, it's best to temper the eggs. You can do this by whisking some of the hot chocolate mixture into the eggs before adding the eggs into the chocolate.

PREP TIME: 30 MINUTES, PLUS 4 HOURS TO CHILL
BAKE TIME: 20 MINUTES
SERVES 6 TO 8

For the crust

¾ cup raw whole natural almonds

¼ cup pecans

½ teaspoon vanilla extract

1 cup pitted Medjool dates

2 tablespoons unsweetened cocoa powder

2 tablespoons coconut oil, melted

2 tablespoons maple syrup

Pinch salt

1 large egg, beaten

For the filling

¼ cup coconut oil

½ cup dairy-free chocolate chunks

¾ cup packed light brown sugar or coconut sugar

3 tablespoons arrowroot

3 large eggs

2 teaspoons vanilla extract

1 cup coconut whipped cream, plus more for serving (page 122)

3 cups raspberries

1. Preheat the oven to 325°F. Lightly coat a 9-inch tart pan with nonstick cooking spray.

2. For the crust, in a food processor on high, pulse the almonds, pecans, and vanilla together until fine crumbs form. Add the dates, cocoa, oil, maple syrup, and salt and pulse until the mixture sticks together. Press into the bottom and sides of the prepared pan. Bake for 15 minutes. Remove from the oven and brush the bottom with the egg. Return to the oven and bake until slightly browned and firm, about 5 minutes. Transfer to a wire rack to cool.

3. For the filling, in a small saucepan over medium-low heat, heat the coconut oil and chocolate chunks together, stirring constantly, until melted. Add the sugar and arrowroot and whisk together until smooth and combined.

4. In a large bowl, using an electric mixer on medium speed, beat the eggs until thick and frothy. Whisk about one-third of the chocolate mixture into the eggs, then whisk the egg mixture into the chocolate mixture in the saucepan. Cook over medium heat for 5 minutes, stirring constantly, until the mixture is thick and glossy and coats the back of a spoon. Remove from the heat and stir in the vanilla. Pour into a bowl and refrigerate until lukewarm, about 30 minutes.

5. Gently fold 1 cup of whipped cream into the chocolate mixture. Cover the remaining whipped cream and refrigerate until serving. Spread the chocolate filling in the crust. Refrigerate for 4 hours before serving.

6. Serve with additional whipped cream and raspberries.

PREP TIP: One way to test the doneness of a custard or other thickened sauces is to dip a spoon into the mixture. The sauce is ready when it coats the back of the spoon. Alternately, run a finger through it and if it leaves a clear path, your custard or sauce is properly thickened. If the path disappears quickly, cook for another few minutes and test again.

STORAGE: Store covered in the refrigerator for up to 3 days.

Summary Vegetable Tart

SOY-FREE

This mouthwatering pie made with roasted tomatoes highlights summer's best produce. You may want to wait until the weekend to prepare this one; although time-consuming, it's worth the effort.

PREP TIME: 1 HOUR AND 20 MINUTES
BAKE TIME: 1 HOUR AND 15 MINUTES
SERVES 8

2 pounds cherry tomatoes

1 tablespoon balsamic vinegar, plus extra for garnish

1 small zucchini, thinly sliced (about 2 cups)

1 small yellow squash, thinly sliced (about 2 cups)

3 teaspoons salt, divided

1 small red onion, thinly sliced

1 tablespoon extra-virgin olive oil

Freshly ground black pepper

1 disk Basic Gluten-Free Pie Dough (page 133)

1 large egg, beaten

8 ounces vegan cream cheese

2 garlic cloves, minced

1 tablespoon chopped fresh basil, plus more for garnish

1 teaspoon chopped fresh thyme (use lemon thyme if possible)

1. Preheat the oven to 400°F. Place a baking sheet on the bottom rack to catch any drippings.

2. Place the tomatoes on a roasting pan and drizzle with the vinegar. Roast until they are soft and lightly charred, about 45 minutes.

3. Meanwhile, in a colander, toss the zucchini and squash with 2 teaspoons of salt. Let drain over the sink for 30 minutes. Gently squeeze out any extra water and transfer to a medium bowl. Add the onion and oil, season with pepper to taste, and toss to combine and coat with the oil.

4. On a floured work surface, roll out the dough to an 11-inch circle. Transfer to a 9-inch pie pan and press into the bottom and sides. Trim the edges, then prick the bottom a few times with a fork. Freeze for 10 minutes.

5. Bake the crust for 20 minutes. Remove from the oven and brush with the beaten egg. Return to the oven and bake until golden, about 10 minutes. Let cool for 10 minutes.

6. In a small bowl, beat the cream cheese, garlic, basil, and thyme together until well blended. Spread over the bottom of the cooled tart. Arrange the zucchini and squash on top, then top the squash with the roasted tomatoes.

7. Bake until the top starts to brown and most of the liquid has evaporated, 35 to 45 minutes. Season with salt and pepper to taste. Garnish with fresh basil and a drizzle of balsamic vinegar.

PREP TIPS:

- Make sure to squeeze as much liquid as possible from the squash and zucchini to prevent a soggy tart.

- Brushing egg onto the crust helps bind it and allows it to crisp.

STORAGE: Store covered in the refrigerator for up to 3 days or in a zip-top plastic bag in the freezer for up to 1 month.

Bacon, Mushroom, and Thyme Quiche

SOY-FREE

Quiches are so versatile. They work for any meal. The beauty of a quiche is that it can be made in advance and reheated just before serving.

PREP TIME: **20 MINUTES**
BAKE TIME: **45 MINUTES**
SERVES 6

1 tablespoon extra-virgin olive oil

2 cups sliced mushrooms

2 teaspoons chopped fresh thyme

1 disk Basic Gluten-Free Pie Dough (page 133)

4 slices turkey bacon or regular bacon

5 large eggs

1 cup plain dairy-free yogurt

¼ teaspoon salt

⅛ teaspoon freshly ground black pepper

Pinch ground nutmeg

1. In a medium nonstick skillet over medium-high heat, heat the oil. Then add the mushrooms and cook, stirring a few times, until tender and the water has evaporated, about 5 minutes. Add the thyme and toss to coat. Remove from the heat.

2. Preheat the oven to 400°F.

3. On a lightly floured work surface, roll out the dough to an 11-inch circle. Transfer to a 9-inch tart pan and press into the bottom and sides. Trim the edges, then prick the bottom a few times with a fork. Bake until golden, about 10 minutes. Transfer to a wire rack to cool. Reduce the oven temperature to 375ºF.

4. In a small skillet over medium-high heat, cook the bacon, turning, until crisp, about 4 minutes. Place between two paper towels to remove extra oil. Set aside.

5. In a large bowl, whisk together the eggs, yogurt, salt, pepper, and nutmeg.

6. Crumble the bacon over the baked piecrust. Top with the mushrooms, then the egg mixture.

7. Bake until a knife inserted in the center comes out clean, 30 to 35 minutes. If the piecrust starts to burn on the edges, tent with aluminum foil and continue baking.

8. Remove from the oven and serve.

REHEATING TIP: If the quiche has been made in advance, cover it with foil and reheat in the oven at 325°F until heated through.

STORAGE: Store covered in the refrigerator for up to 3 days.

Spinach and Sun-Dried Tomato Potato-Crusted Quiche

NUT-FREE | SOY-FREE

Using potatoes for the crust is a tasty twist on a typical quiche and adds more nutritious veggies to the meal.

PREP TIME: **25 MINUTES**
BAKE TIME: **1 HOUR**
SERVES 4 TO 6

2 or 3 large Yukon Gold potatoes, thinly sliced

½ cup drained and chopped oil-packed sun-dried tomatoes, plus 3 tablespoons reserved oil, divided

5 large eggs

1½ cups plain dairy-free yogurt

¼ cup cornstarch

½ teaspoon salt

¼ teaspoon freshly ground black pepper

1 tablespoon chopped fresh basil

Pinch ground nutmeg

⅓ cup chopped scallions (green parts only)

1 cup chopped spinach

1. Preheat the oven to 450°F. Place a baking sheet on the bottom rack to catch any drippings. Lightly coat a 9-inch pie pan with nonstick cooking spray.

2. Line the bottom and sides of the pan with the potato slices. Drizzle with 2 tablespoons of reserved oil from the tomatoes. Bake until slightly browned, about 10 minutes. Transfer to a wire rack to cool.

3. Reduce the oven temperature to 350°F.

4. In a large bowl, whisk together the eggs, yogurt, cornstarch, salt, pepper, basil, and nutmeg. Stir in the scallions, tomatoes, and remaining 1 tablespoon of reserved oil.

5. Scatter the spinach over the potato slices. Top with the egg mixture.

6. Bake until a knife inserted in the center comes out clean, 50 to 60 minutes. Let cool on a wire rack for 20 minutes before slicing.

PREP TIP: Make sure the potato slices overlap slightly to fully cover the bottom of the pie pan.

STORAGE: Store covered in the refrigerator for up to 3 days.

SUBSTITUTIONS: Substitute kale for the spinach. For a little extra sweetness, use sweet potatoes instead of the Yukon potatoes.

Chicken-Mushroom Pot Pie

SOY-FREE

My favorite comfort foods are one-dish meals, like this perennial favorite. Feel free to change up the vegetables. For example, use red onion instead of scallion, red pepper instead of carrots, and fennel in place of celery.

PREP TIME: **30 MINUTES**
BAKE TIME: **45 MINUTES**
SERVES 8

1 tablespoon extra-virgin olive oil
2 cups chopped carrots
1 cup chopped scallions (green and white parts)
1 cup sliced mushrooms
¾ cup thinly sliced celery
1 tablespoon chopped fresh rosemary
1 teaspoon poultry seasoning
1 cup unsweetened dairy-free milk
1½ cups chicken broth
4 tablespoons vegan butter
⅓ cup cornstarch
¾ teaspoon salt
¼ teaspoon freshly ground pepper
2 chicken breasts, cooked and diced
1 cup frozen peas
¼ cup chopped fresh parsley
1 disk Basic Gluten-Free Pie Dough (page 133)
Pinch granulated sugar

PREP TIP: If the dough becomes too warm to handle, spread it on a floured sheet of parchment paper, transfer to a baking pan, and freeze for 5 to 10 minutes.

STORAGE: Store covered in the refrigerator for up to 3 days.

1. Preheat the oven to 350°F.

2. In a medium saucepan, heat the oil over medium-high heat, Add the carrots, scallions, mushrooms, and celery and cook, stirring, until the vegetables are tender, about 10 minutes. Stir in the rosemary and poultry seasoning. Transfer to a large bowl.

3. In the same saucepan, whisk together the milk, broth, butter, arrowroot, salt, and pepper. Over medium heat, bring to a simmer and cook, whisking, until it starts to thicken, about 10 minutes. Carefully add to the bowl with the vegetables. Stir the chicken, peas, and parsley into the bowl with the sauce. Pour into a 9-inch pie pan.

4. On a lightly floured work surface, roll out the dough to a 10-inch circle. Place over the chicken mixture and crimp the edges. Cut a few slashes in the crust to allow steam to escape.

5. Bake until the crust is golden brown and the filling is bubbly, about 40 to 45 minutes. Let cool for 10 minutes before serving.

Warm Peach Cobbler

CONTAINS COCONUT | SOY-FREE

Like many of the celebration desserts in this book, this cobbler is bursting with ripe fruit. It's best during the summer months when peaches are at their peak. Bring it to barbecues, parties, or any gathering when you need a simple dessert, and serve with dairy-free vanilla ice cream or coconut whipped cream (see page 122).

PREP TIME: **20 MINUTES**
BAKE TIME: **25 MINUTES**
SERVES 6 TO 8

For the filling

8 large ripe peaches, pitted and cut into small chunks

¼ cup maple syrup

2½ tablespoons arrowroot or cornstarch

2 tablespoons freshly squeezed lemon juice

1 teaspoon ground nutmeg

1 teaspoon ground cinnamon

1 teaspoon vanilla extract

⅓ cup packed light brown sugar or coconut sugar

1. Preheat the oven to 400°F. Lightly coat a 9-inch square baking pan with nonstick cooking spray.

2. For the filling, in a large bowl, stir together the peaches, maple syrup, arrowroot, lemon juice, nutmeg, cinnamon, and vanilla. Place in the prepared pan. Sprinkle with the sugar. Bake for 10 minutes.

For the topping

1 cup plus 1 tablespoon Basic Gluten-Free Flour Blend (page 10) or store-bought equivalent

½ cup granulated sugar, divided

1 tablespoon psyllium husk

1¼ teaspoons baking powder

½ teaspoon xanthan gum

½ teaspoon salt

¼ teaspoon baking soda

6 tablespoons coconut oil, chilled until very solid

⅓ cup vanilla dairy-free yogurt

2 tablespoons water

1 large egg white, beaten

3. For the topping, in a large bowl, whisk together the flour blend, ¼ cup of the sugar, the psyllium husk, baking powder, xanthan gum, salt, and baking soda. Using a pastry blender or two knives, cut in the oil until crumbly with pea-size chunks. With a fork, stir in the yogurt and water just until moist and somewhat sticky.

4. Carefully spoon the topping over the peaches. Cover as evenly as possible, leaving just a few open spots. Brush the top with the egg white and sprinkle with the remaining ¼ cup of sugar.

5. Bake until the fruit is bubbling and a toothpick inserted in the center comes out clean, 10 to 15 minutes. Transfer to a wire rack to cool.

STORAGE: Store covered in the refrigerator for up to 3 days.

VARIATION: Turn this into plum or nectarine cobbler using the same amount of fruit as the peaches.

Apple-Cranberry Crumble

SOY-FREE | VEGAN

This is one of the simplest desserts when you need to make something quickly. Serve warm with a scoop of dairy-free vanilla ice cream.

PREP TIME: 15 MINUTES
BAKE TIME: 45 MINUTES
SERVES 8 TO 10

3 medium Pink Lady apples, cored, peeled, and finely chopped

2 cups fresh or frozen cranberries

1 tablespoon granulated sugar

1 teaspoon ground cinnamon

1½ cups certified gluten-free rolled oats

¼ cup Basic Gluten-Free Flour Blend (page 10) or store-bought equivalent

½ cup packed light brown sugar or coconut sugar

½ cup chopped walnuts or pecans

½ cup maple syrup or honey

½ cup coconut oil, melted

Pinch salt

1. Preheat the oven to 350°F. Lightly coat a 9-inch square baking pan with nonstick cooking spray.

2. In a large bowl, stir together the apples, cranberries, granulated sugar, and cinnamon until well blended. Pour into the prepared pan.

3. In a food processor, pulse the oats, flour blend, brown sugar, walnuts, maple syrup, oil, and salt one or two times to mix gently, but do not process the oats too finely. Crumble the oat mixture evenly over the apples.

4. Bake until the topping starts to brown and the fruit bubbles, 40 to 45 minutes. Serve slightly warm or chilled.

STORAGE: Store covered at room temperature for up to 3 days.

SUBSTITUTIONS: You can turn this into an apple crumble by using five to six apples and omitting the cranberries.

Coconut-Raisin Baked Rice Pudding

CONTAINS COCONUT | SOY-FREE

This tropical custard pudding is a beloved treat best served chilled.

PREP TIME: **15 MINUTES, PLUS 2 HOURS TO CHILL**

BAKE TIME: **50 MINUTES**

SERVES 6 TO 8

3 cups cooked rice, cooled

½ cup raisins

2 (13.5-ounce) cans full-fat coconut milk

¾ cup granulated sugar

3 large eggs

½ cup unsweetened shredded coconut

2 teaspoons vanilla extract

1½ teaspoons ground cinnamon

1 teaspoon cornstarch

Grated zest from 1 small lemon (½ teaspoon)

¼ teaspoon ground nutmeg

¼ teaspoon salt

1. Place a large roasting pan filled halfway with water in the oven. Preheat the oven to 350°F. Lightly coat a 9-inch square baking pan with nonstick cooking spray.

2. Sprinkle the cooked rice evenly in the prepared pan. Top with the raisins.

3. In a large bowl, whisk the coconut milk, sugar, eggs, coconut, vanilla, cinnamon, cornstarch, lemon zest, nutmeg, and salt together. Pour over the rice and raisins.

4. Carefully place the baking pan in the roasting pan in the oven; the water should reach halfway up the sides of the baking pan. Bake until slightly browned and a knife inserted in the center comes out clean, 40 to 50 minutes.

5. Remove from the water bath and place the square pan on a wire rack to cool. Cover and refrigerate for at least 2 hours before serving.

STORAGE: Store covered in the refrigerator for up to 5 days.

VARIATION: Place sliced mango on the pudding once cooled.

MEASUREMENT CONVERSIONS

Volume Equivalents (Liquid)

US STANDARD	US STANDARD (ounces)	METRIC (approximate)
2 tablespoons	1 fl. oz.	30 mL
¼ cup	2 fl. oz.	60 mL
½ cup	4 fl. oz.	120 mL
1 cup	8 fl. oz.	240 mL
1½ cups	12 fl. oz.	355 mL
2 cups or 1 pint	16 fl. oz.	475 mL
4 cups or 1 quart	32 fl. oz.	1 L
1 gallon	128 fl. oz.	4 L

Oven Temperatures

FAHRENHEIT (F)	CELSIUS (C) (approximate)
250°F	120°C
300°F	150°C
325°F	165°C
350°F	180°C
375°F	190°C
400°F	200°C
425°F	220°C
450°F	230°C

Volume Equivalents (Dry)

US STANDARD	METRIC (approximate)
⅛ teaspoon	0.5 mL
¼ teaspoon	1 mL
½ teaspoon	2 mL
¾ teaspoon	4 mL
1 teaspoon	5 mL
1 tablespoon	15 mL
¼ cup	59 mL
⅓ cup	79 mL
½ cup	118 mL
⅔ cup	156 mL
¾ cup	177 mL
1 cup	235 mL
2 cups or 1 pint	475 mL
3 cups	700 mL
4 cups or 1 quart	1 L

Weight Equivalents

US STANDARD	METRIC (approximate)
½ ounce	15 g
1 ounce	30 g
2 ounces	60 g
4 ounces	115 g
8 ounces	225 g
12 ounces	340 g
16 ounces or 1 pound	455 g

iNDEX

ACKNOWLEDGMENTS

This is a book that has been in the works for years, only I didn't know it. My best recipes have come from my readers and family, who suggest ideas for their favorite recipes they want made healthier and/or gluten-free. Those early years of testing and working with gluten-free baking were often frustrating, but I never gave up. As a result, I developed new techniques that began yielding great results, which led, finally, to this book.

I acknowledge so many people who made this book happen. To my publisher, Callisto Media, and my wonderful editor, Pam Kingsley, and the rest of the team who worked hard to put this book together with me.

Special thanks to my husband, Kristopher, who has always supported me, and encourages me to never give up. He made this happen through a lot of recipe taste testing and by watching our kids so I could bake and write.

To my two boys, Chase and Curren. You are the best at constructive criticism! You inspire me every day with the recipes I develop and inspire healthy living for families everywhere.

Huge thanks to my mom, Diane, who taught me all about baking techniques and has always encouraged me to live my dreams.

To God, for making my manifestations and dreams a reality, because I can do all things through Christ who gives me strength.

And last but not least, to you, my readers. This is for you because you can do all things, even when you might not feel like you can. You can cook, you can bake, you can heal, and you can thrive. I hope these recipes give you the encouragement and fuel you need to live your best life.

ABOUT THE AUTHOR

 **DANIELLE FAHRENKRUG** is a healthy living, whole-food advocate dedicated to helping others regain and maintain their health and vibrance through healing, whole-food recipes. She specializes in creating simple and delicious gluten-free recipes the whole family will enjoy, while educating readers on the benefits of the specific foods and ingredients in each recipe. If you want to learn more about the healing powers of food and new, healthy, simple recipe ideas, visit her blog: DelightfulMomFood.com. You can also find her on Instagram, Facebook, and Pinterest (@delightfulmomfood). She lives in Buellton, California, with her husband and two boys.

Printed in the USA
CPSIA information can be obtained
at www.ICGtesting.com
CBHW041934260324
5882CB00002B/8

9 781641 529129